PLOVERS

PLOVERS

by

RICHARD VAUGHAN

TERENCE DALTON LIMITED
LAVENHAM . SUFFOLK
1980

Published by
TERENCE DALTON LIMITED

ISBN 0 900963 36 0

All photographs by the author

Text photoset in 11/12pt. Baskerville

Printed in Great Britain at
THE LAVENHAM PRESS LIMITED
LAVENHAM . SUFFOLK

Contents

Index of Illustrations

CHAPTER ONE

The World's Plovers

ON THE whole, the plovers constitute a homogeneous group, and most experts are agreed as to exactly which birds belong to the plover family or *Charadriidae*. It is one of the nine families of so-called waders, of which there are 190 species in all: 63 of them belong to the plover family and 82 to the only other large wader family, the sandpipers and curlews. By avian standards the plover family is not a large one; there are 82 gull species (*Laridae*), 395 warblers (*Sylviidae*) and—largest of all—436 finches (*Fringillidae*). Closely related to the plovers but nowadays usually placed in the sandpiper family is the turnstone *Arenaria interpres*. Definitely not plovers, in spite of their names, are the Norfolk plover or stone curlew *Burhinus oedicnemus,* which has a family of its own, the *Burhinidae*; the Egyptian plover *Pluvianus aegyptius*, which is a courser and belongs to the *Glareolidae* family; and the crab-plover *Dromas ardeola* of the Indian Ocean which lays a single white egg at the end of a long burrow and is of the *Dronadidae* family.

Plovers are small or medium sized waders ranging from six to over fifteen inches in length, with rather short or medium length legs and shortish bills, usually shorter than the head. They feed mainly by surface pecking rather than digging; many species are adept at pulling out worms. Present throughout the world in bare open areas and along shores, plovers walk or run, often swiftly, they are gregarious, and many species are migratory. The nest is a hollow in the ground, usually with little lining, and the two-five eggs are buff or grey with black spots and blotches. The young leave the nest and run immediately after hatching, and both sexes look after them. Though few plovers are brightly coloured—black, brown, grey and white are predominant—the plumage of most is boldly patterned; that of females differs only slightly from males. The back colour is cryptic, being correlated with ground colour—plovers living in sandy areas have sandy coloured backs.

Although, as we have said, there has never been much difficulty in deciding which birds belong to the plover family, ornithologists are very far from agreement when it comes to sorting the plovers into genera. At first there was no problem—the family was split into two groups each of which was regarded as constituting a genus: *Charadrius* and *Vanellus*. But in the nineteenth century the pendulum swung the other way, and the experts began to increase the number of genera until almost every species which had previously been labelled *Vanellus* was given a genus of its own. The golden and grey plovers were placed in different genera because of a difference in skull shape which was subsequently shown not to have anything to do with their relationship. On the contrary it was found to be solely due to a difference of habitat: the golden plover is mainly a fresh-water bird and therefore has small nasal glands and well ossified suborbital rims, while the grey plover frequents salt water and therefore has poorly ossified rims. Then again, the grey plover's hind toe, lacking in the golden plover and most other plovers, was thought to indicate its isolation from other plovers, meriting its placing in a separate genus. Nowadays, however, most experts consider this character unimportant in determining relationships; they regard the hind toe as something which has outgrown its usefulness and is on the way out; when exactly the right mutations occur to occasion its disappearance in one species or other is purely a matter of chance. Other characteristics of *Vanellus*-type plovers, the wattle between eye and bill, the spur at the bend of the wing, the crest, are present in some species and not in others, but are not now regarded as necessarily generically determinant. Against their variety must be set the fact that the characteristic black-and-white wing and tail pattern is maintained with remarkable constancy throughout the group of *Vanellus* plovers. In the case of the *Charadrius* -type plovers, the disruptive marks formed by the breast bands and head markings, among other things, have persuaded recent workers to place all the species in a single genus.

Bock, whose review of the plovers was published in 1958, reverted to the original idea and divided the family into two large genera of equal size, *Vanellus* and *Charadrius*, each containing 24 species and four smaller genera. The typical *Vanellus* plover is the familiar lapwing *Vanellus vanellus*; the typical *Charadrius* plover is the ringed plover *Charadrius hiaticula*. Then come two small, outlying genera, *Pluvialis* containing the golden and grey plovers, and *Eudromias* made up of the two dotterel species. Finally there are two "oddities" which seemed to demand genera entirely to themselves: the New Zealand wrybill, which however is closely related to *Charadrius*, and the Magellanic plover, found only in Tierra del Fuego.

The ancestor of *Vanellus* plovers probably originated in Africa. From this centre of distribution there seem to have been some five separate "invasions" of Eurasia, one of them giving rise to our lapwing, and another, indirectly, to the two species in Australia, and two separate invasions of South America across the Atlantic, giving rise to the three species there. There are no *Vanellus* plovers in North America. As to the *Charadrius* plovers, their distribution is genuinely world wide and hard to elucidate in historical terms. They do fall naturally into three large groups: the ringed plovers, the sand plovers typified by the Kentish plover *Charadrius alexandrinus*, and the mountain or plains plovers, which seem to have evolved from a Kentish plover type ancestor. Outside these groups are four somewhat isolated species.

The distribution of plovers throughout the world poses some extremely complex problems, which can only be touched on here. Take the dotterels, for example. There are only two species of *Eudromias*, the migratory *morinellus* of north European and Asiatic mountains and tundra which will be considered at length later, and *ruficollis*, a resident of the mountains and plains of South America. The two species are extremely similar in size and plumage and in other respects; how on earth can one explain the enormous gap between their ranges? A similar puzzle is provided by two species of sand plover, close relatives of the Kentish plover. *Charadrius falklandicus* is found in South America; *Charadrius bicinctus* inhabits New Zealand. In spite of the many thousands of miles of open ocean between the ranges of the two birds, they are almost identical except for the colour of the lower of the two breast bands, which is black in one and red in the other. It is not even clear that they really are two distinct species. One explanation is that at some time in the past, when Antarctica was not ice-covered, their common ancestor lived there, perhaps migrating northwards in the autumn. There are in fact ten species of southern hemisphere plover which today have limited ranges in the very southernmost tips of the southern land masses. Perhaps these are all relict populations of species that were frozen out of Antarctica long ago.

In this brief account of the plovers of the world, we shall not describe the European and other species which are the subject of later chapters of this book. It so happens that these species, which Britain and western Europe hold as residents or common migrants, are a very representative selection of plovers, including the typical *Vanellus* plover in our familiar lapwing, the dotterel, one of the two members of the genus *Eudromias*, the ringed plover, little ringed plover and Kentish plover, typical representatives of two groups of *Charadrius* plovers, and two of the four *Pluvialis* plovers, the golden and grey plovers. Add to these the rarer species, dealt with in Chapter Twelve, which have turned up in Britain or may well do so, namely an Asiatic *Vanellus* now usually placed in the genus *Chettusia*, the sociable plover; three more *Charadrius* plovers—the American killdeer (*vociferous*), and the Asiatic Caspian plover (*asiaticus*) and greater sand plover (*leschenaultii*); and an African *Vanellus* plover—the spur-winged (*spinosus*); and we are left with the task, in this chapter, of dealing with the remaining plovers of North America, Africa, Asia and those of the southern hemisphere.

As to North American plovers, that continent is relatively poor in species. It shares the ringed plover with Europe, though the North American ringed plover has been given subspecific or specific status because of the greater extent of webbing on its feet (*semipalmatus*) (Smith 1969). Moreover, North America shares the lesser golden plover *Pluvialis dominica* with Asia; its black-bellied plover is our grey plover; its killdeer has strayed to Europe and therefore features in Chapter Twelve, and its snowy plover is our Kentish plover. This leaves three other species of *Charadrius* plover: the very pale brown piping plover (*melodus*) which breeds on the east coast and locally inland, to which we shall return in Chapter Twelve; the larger Wilson's plover (*wilsonia*) which breeds in the same general area but only on coastal islands between Virginia and Texas; and *montanus*, the upland or mountain plover. So much for North American plovers.

In what follows, rather than trying to describe or even mention every species, a selection of the world's plovers only will be considered. We shall not for example have anything more to say of the South American dotterel, nor shall we dwell on the one other member of the genus *Pluvialis* not so far mentioned, namely *obscura* from New Zealand, which differs from its relatives in having reddish, not black, underparts. Nor shall we devote space to discussing the two Australian lapwings, the large masked plover *Vanellus miles,* which has well-developed wing spurs, and the banded plover *V. tricolor*, which has a black cap, a white line across the head through the eye, a yellow-rimmed eye with a small red wattle, and a black band extending from the eye down the neck and across the breast.

Only one *Vanellus* -type plover lacks the black and white tail typical of the genus—the white-tailed plover *Chettusia leucura*; but this pale brownish bird, lapwing-sized, with long yellow legs, displays the characteristic *Vanellus* black and white wing pattern when the bird is in flight. Its breeding range extends from Syria in the west, through Iraq and Iran into the Soviet Union south and east of the Caspian and Aral Seas. It leaves this rather limited area at the end of the summer and winters mainly in Egypt and the Nile valley in the west and along the shores of the Persian Gulf and in north-east India in the east. Stragglers have occurred in France and Algeria, and the white-tailed plover has been recorded at least four times from Malta. The first example was found in the game stall of the market there on 18th October 1864; the second and third were shot (!) on 24th October 1869 and 22nd October 1973. In 1975 one turned up in Britain.

The white tailed plover, in spite of its restricted range, is a common bird where suitable terrain occurs. It breeds on swampy lakes and river shores and on deltas and islands in lakes, laying four pear-shaped eggs in a depression, usually in a fairly open situation, in the last third of April. It is a noisy bird which calls loudly "chetyre, chetyre, chetyre"—the Russian word for four.

Another Asiatic lapwing is the red-wattled plover *V. indicus,* which has a black and white head and breast, yellow legs, brown back and a bright red wattle in front of its eyes. Its Russian name is "Indian decorated lapwing" but in fact its range extends from Arabia right across India to Vietnam. It is resident and often numerous in the south of its range, which only just extends into the Soviet Union in eastern Turkmania. A related species, the Chinese decorated lapwing *V. cinereus,* has a yellow wattle and nests in Japan, Korea, Mongolia, and China from central Manchuria to the Yangtze River.

While Eurasia has some half-dozen species of *Vanellus* plover, of which we have mentioned five, Africa has twelve. One of the most handsome and conspicuous is the blacksmith plover *Vanellus armatus,* so called because of its loud ringing "tik tik" or "klink klink" call, which sounds rather like two pieces of metal being struck together or a smith hitting his anvil. It is closely related to the spur-winged plover, and has a rather similar black and white plumage pattern except for its white crown, black on sides of throat and black patch on the back. It occurs locally in marshy areas from southern Kenya southwards, breeding from April to August in Kenya and from September onwards in South Africa. Another handsome African *Vanellus* is the crowned plover (*coronatus*), which has uniform grey-brown upperparts with a white ring round its head above the eye, and black in the centre of the crown; the legs are red and the bill black and red. It is well distributed through Central, East and South Africa on grassy plains and in open bush country, and lays only two or three eggs, buffish or yellowish brown in ground colour, finely speckled with dark brown, The wattled plover *V. senegallus* is a large African lapwing with brown plumage except for its white forehead, black chin and black-streaked throat. It has two elongated wattles between the eye and bill on either side, one red and one yellow, and is found throughout Africa except the Congo forests and the extreme southwest. One African *Vanellus,* besides the spur-winged plover, has wandered to the eastern Mediterranean, the blackhead plover, *V. tectus* or, as some would have it, *Sarciphorus tectus,* which breeds right across the continent from Senegal to Eritrea, inhabiting dry plains. It is partly migratory, has a small red wattle and a crest, and is very like a brown-backed long-legged lapwing.

Just as Africa is richer in *Vanellus*-type plovers than any other part of the world so it is probably the best place to see *Charadrius* plovers. In East and South Africa, for example, one might hope to find at least four or five species of *Charadrius* breeding, while with any luck along the coast in winter one could add a further five or six species, including both sand plovers, and the ringed and little ringed plovers; and inland one would find the Caspian plover. Of the breeding species, the local chestnut-banded sand plover *Charadrius venustus* nests on the shores of three lakes in Kenya and Tanzania and is resident there; Forbes's plover *Ch. forbesi* is even rarer. Three other species are widespread breeders. The white-fronted sand plover *Ch. marginatus* breeds on sandy coasts and river and lake shores in East and Central Africa and Madagascar. It is a predominantly pale bird, brown above and white below with a reddish-brown breast and a white forehead. The three eggs are laid in a depression in the sand, and incubated in the normal way, but when the bird leaves them it almost covers them with sand, making the nest extremely hard to find (Hall 1960). The three-banded plover *Ch. tricollaris* is not unlike the ringed plover but has no black on the head and two narrow, instead of one broad, black bands across the breast, and is mainly found inland, almost always near water. Kittlitz's sand plover *Ch. pecuarius* is common throughout Africa except in the forests and deserts. It has buff or rufous underparts, a black line through the eye and white eye-stripes above it which meet at the back of the neck to form a collar. It too covers its eggs with sand, but has a clutch of only two.

Exceptionally well camouflaged in their usual habitat of pebbles, these newly-hatched ringed plover chicks are somewhat conspicuous on the bare concrete of an old airfield runway. The female is brooding one chick while two others crouch near her.

Before concluding this brief review of the world's plovers, we ought to make special mention of three rather rare and unusual species.

The shore plover *Charadrius novaeseelandiae* is distinct enough from other *Charadrius* plovers to have been placed by some ornithologists in a genus of its own, *Thinornis*. It differs from most of them in having a rather thinner bill, and instead of a dark breast band, it has a black collar round its neck which includes the cheek, throat and forehead, but which narrows at the back of the neck. The brownish-grey crown is separated from this black area by a narrow white stripe. Apart from this nearly black head, the shore plover is greyish-brown above and white below; its bill and legs are orange-pink. It was apparently widespread around the coasts of New Zealand during most of the nineteenth century but by 1900 or so it had disappeared altogether from the mainland, and is now found only on one of the Chatham Islands, some five hundred miles east of New Zealand, far out in the open Pacific. The world population of under 100 pairs is thus concentrated on a single small island. The oddest, un-plover-like feature of the shore plover is its nest, which is placed in a horizontal hole or short tunnel, among stones, underground, or in or under thick vegetation. It is lined with grass and two or three eggs are laid between November and February.

The wrybill plover *Anarhynchus frontalis* is another species confined to New Zealand, where it breeds in South Island and winters in and around three large estuaries in North Island. The population has been estimated at about 5,000 individuals. The wrybill is, to all intents and purposes, a typical *Charadrius* plover. A little larger than a ringed plover, it is grey above and white below and, in the breeding season, it has a black band across the breast. But a curious and quite unique feature has persuaded all the experts to keep it in a genus of its own: the rather long, for a plover, black bill is curved towards the right near the tip, at an angle of about 12 degrees. So far nobody has come up with an explanation as to the origin and purpose of this curious feature. How exactly is it advantageous for feeding on the shingle banks of rivers which the wrybill frequents in summer or in the estuary mud in winter?

The last of the world's plover species to be mentioned here is also one of the rarest and most interesting. The Magellanic plover *Pluvianellus socialis* may indeed not be a plover at all—its short legs and straight, sharp bill, make it possible that it is related more closely to the turnstones. It is grey above and white below, and it has a brownish breast band. The tail is brown-black, edged with white; the legs are pink and the eyes crimson. The Magellanic plover breeds on the shores of the Straits of Magellan and winters north in Argentina. Very few ornithologists have seen it alive and the chick in down has never been described. Only two eggs are laid, in a scrape in shingle on the shore or on bare ground.

CHAPTER TWO

Plovers in History, Literature and Legend

THE exact meaning of the name plover has long been disputed, though the origin of the word from Latin *pluvia*, rain, probably via *pluviarius*, is clear. The problem is, why should the plover be a "rain bird"? As to which species of plover is actually meant, there can be little doubt that the word refers to the golden plover. This bird is called plover, *plevier*, *piviere*, *pluvier* in English, Dutch, Italian and French, with the epithet golden added and, except in English and Dutch, names other than plover (or *plevier*) are used for the ringed plover, lapwing and other species. Since we are dealing with a Romance word, the assumption is that it was the Italians (or Romans) who first named the golden plover "rain bird", though it is remarkable that there is no mention of the plover in Pliny's *Natural history*. If this was the case, then a possible explanation is that the bird was called rain bird because its annual arrival in the Mediterranean area and especially Italy, where it does not breed, coincided with the autumn rains. On the other hand, this cannot apply so well in Germany, where the golden plover does breed. There, it and all the other plovers except the lapwing are called *Regenpfeifer* or rain-piper, again with a suitable epithet. As a matter of fact, few of the European names of plover species are genuinely descriptive: among the most apt are the Italian *corriere*, meaning "runner", for the ringed plover, and the Swedish *fjällpipare* or fell-piper for the dotterel. The lapwing is named, more often than not, after its call: in Dutch *kievit* and in German *Kiebitz;* in Norwegian *vipe* and in Danish *vibe*.

Spencer (1953) made a detailed study of the lapwing's English names; while Swainson listed local names of all the plovers. The name lapwing, which in Middle English had four syllables, *lappewinke*, is said to be derived from *leapan* to leap and *winken* to turn and twist. It was used by most of the early ornithological writers and, as we shall see, by Chaucer, Shakespeare and other famous authors. On the other hand, though it remains the standard English name for the species, Spencer found that it scarcely figured at all among local names. Throughout the Midlands and the south of England, "peewit" reigned supreme, while in Lancashire "tewit" was dominant, in East Yorkshire "teupit", and in parts of southern Scotland "peesweep", were the usual names. "Teuchet" is found in Kincardine, Banff and Aberdeenshire, and throughout

Ringed plover incubating.

"Northern" golden plover at nest

"Southern" golden plover near nest

Ireland "green plover" is the most commonly used name. Nor should it go unremarked that the lapwing is often simply called "plover". Names that are apparently dying out are "piewipe" in Lincolnshire and "horniwink" in Devon.

Bones of plovers of any species seem to be rare or even non-existent in British Iron Age and Roman sites; nor have they been found at all commonly in medieval excavations. One interesting record is from the Late Saxon period: at Portchester Castle in Hampshire, bones of the golden plover, among those of other waders, have been identified (Society of Antiquaries 1975). Presumably the birds were eaten and must have been netted on passage or as winter visitors—surely not shot with bow and arrow? There is another record of a golden plover from the Saxon period (about 650 to about 850 AD)—a bone was found at North Elmham in Norfolk (Wilson 1976). Bones of grey and golden plovers have been excavated at King's Lynn, Norfolk, in an area where both species are common at the present day; and lapwing remains have been found there too. While the plovers dated from the middle ages, the lapwing was post-medieval (Clarke and Carter 1977). A single lapwing, among teal, curlew and woodcock remains, was excavated from a medieval cesspit in Cuckoo Lane, Southampton, dating from the thirteenth or early fourteenth century (Platt and Coleman-Smith 1975). These records are few and far between: there is no question that many others will be published by archaeologists in the next few decades.

In the middle ages and early modern period there are a number of literary references to lapwing. Geoffrey Chaucer refers to it in his *Parliament of fowls* of 1382 (Baugh 1963): "The false lapwynge, ful of trecherye", perhaps alluding to the bird's injury feigning antics, though these are not, in fact, very common. More likely, the lapwing's supposed treachery was derived from the way it flies overhead calling loudly and so distracts the intruder from the nest. By 1600 or so quite a number of literary allusions can be found to the lapwing calling most loudly when the intruder is furthest from the nest. This widespread belief explains why Gower calls it "the bird falsest of all", and it also explains the line "far from her nest the lapwing cries away" in *A comedy of errors*. Indeed the lapwing was almost synonymous with deceit, in the popular estimation, in the period 1350-1650. Two fifteenth-century authors, indulging in what was then a quite popular pastime of drawing up lists of collective nouns, include the lapwing. *The Boke of St Albans*, printed in 1486, has a "desserte of lapwyngs"; the Bodleian Library MS (in Oxford) Digby 196 has a "deseyte of lapewynkes". Who ever heard of a desert of lapwings? Obviously the *Boke of St Albans* got it wrong while Digby 196, though with eccentric spelling, is right: it was a deceit of lapwings.

Another belief about the lapwing prevalent around 1600 was the curious one that the chicks run away from the nest so soon after hatching that they still have the egg-shell on their heads. Shakespeare mentions this too, in *Hamlet*:

"The lapwing runs away with the shell on his head." Spencer (1953) found five allusions to this in English writers between 1602 and 1638.

Another source of information about early birds is provided by household and other accounts, which mention plovers and other birds eaten, and descriptions of banquets. There cannot be any reasonable doubt that the seven *upupae* bought for 2d each for a dinner at Oxford in 1395 were in fact lapwings, and it seems likely that the "plovers" on sale in London at this date were also lapwings, though the possibility that they were golden plovers cannot be ruled out. Unspecified plovers were eaten at King Henry VI's coronation banquet in 1422. At Hunstanton in Norfolk the sixteenth-century household accounts of the le Straunge family frequently record the purchase of plovers; in an entry for 15th November 1548 there is a mention of "a green plover j [penny]", which may indicate that all these plovers were lapwings except this one which was probably a golden plover. One remarkable entry for 15th November 1523 records payment "for a Woodcocke, a grey plover and a Snype, iiid" (Gurney 1921). This must be the earliest definite mention of a grey plover in any English source and probably anywhere; the Shuttleworth accounts for Lancashire mention lapwings and a grey plover brought home in June, but this was at the end of the sixteenth century.

A lapwing calls while flying over an intruder's head.

It is perhaps not surprising that early paintings of plovers are extremely rare; indeed the only British plover to occur in medieval art seems to be the lapwing. No doubt the others were either too small and unfamiliar, like the ringed plover, or else too nondescript to be easily recognizable, like the golden plover. Even such a distinctive and apparently common bird as the lapwing appears only occasionally in medieval manuscript illuminations. A handsomely illustrated thirteenth-century manuscript in the Vatican Library (Pal. lat. 1071), written for the emperor Frederick II of Hohenstaufen, of his treatise *On the art of hunting with birds*, that is falconry, has numerous paintings of birds in its margins, including several accurate lapwings both in flight and at rest. The book was illustrated in southern Italy or Sicily around 1240 and presumably the lapwing was only known there, then as now, as a winter visitor and passage migrant. More interesting from our point of view is a painting of an unmistakable lapwing in an illustrated bestiary or book of beasts which follows on in the same manuscript after a richly-illuminated psalter known as the Peterborough Psalter. This book, now in the library of Corpus Christi College, Cambridge (MS 53), was almost certainly produced in East Anglia around 1310. Noteworthy is the fact that the lapwing illustrates the text relating to the hoopoe, or *upupa* in Latin, which seems to indicate that the artist did not know the hoopoe but simply drew the only bird he knew with a conspicuous crest, for the bird in the text is described as having a prominent crest. This, of course, if true, would confirm the attribution of the book on stylistic and other grounds to England, where the hoopoe is, and probably was then, extremely rare, if not quite unknown. Another recognizable lapwing is to be found in the fourteenth-century Holkham Bible Picture Book (Yapp 1979).

One of the most interesting early collections of bird paintings in Europe, though it dates from well after the close of the middle ages, was made by a Strasbourg fisherman called Leonhard Baldner (Gurney 1921). Several versions exist of his illustrated book of paintings of birds, fishes and animals, dating from between 1653 and 1666. Of the fifty or more specifically identifiable birds in the British Library MS (Addit. MSS. 6485 and 6486) of Baldner's work, four are plovers: the lapwing, golden plover, ringed plover and Kentish plover.

It is interesting to compare Baldner's first-hand knowledge of plovers, reflected in his paintings, with the knowledge of plovers of the foremost British naturalist of those days, Sir Thomas Browne, who drew up his account of birds and fishes in 1662 (Stevenson 1870). Sir Thomas, who lived in Norwich, knew the golden plover: "they breed not with us, but in some parts of Scotland, and plentifully in Ireland". He also knew the ringed plover well, calling it the "ringelstones", and describing it as "common about Yarmouth sands, laying its eggs about June in the sand and shingle". Naturally, he knew the lapwing, but it is interesting to find he was familiar with the dotterel too. "The *morinellus* or dotterel, about Thetford and the Champian, comes to us in September and March, staying not long, and is an excellent dish".

Sir Thomas Browne's knowledge of plovers, scanty as it evidently was, was a good deal more substantial than that of his predecessor of a hundred years or more before his time, the sixteenth-century naturalist Dr William Turner. His Latin treatise entitled *A short and succinct history of the principal birds noticed by Pliny and Aristotle* was published in Cologne in 1544 (Evans 1903). Although most of his life was devoted to religious controversy, this Protestant divine found time to acquire a knowledge of birds much superior to that of any other English writer of his day except, perhaps, his contemporary Dr John Kay or Caius, the scholar who refounded Gonville and Caius College, Cambridge, which had been founded as Gonville Hall in 1348 by Edmund Gonville; he was also King Edward VI's physician. Turner describes only two species of plover, the golden plover and the lapwing. Aristotle's *pardalus* he identifies as the English "pluver", in German *eyn pulver*, a bird which "runs very swiftly, and by its cry mimics the whistle which shepherds and post-boys make with pouting lips. It has the feathers almost ash-colour, each sprinkled with one yellow spot . . . " This could only be the golden plover. As to the lapwing, Turner is at pains to distinguish it from the *upupa* or hoopoe, of which he gives an accurate description, having evidently seen it in Germany. He points out that the hoopoe is never seen in Britain, and that the bird which British writers call *upupa* is there called, in English, lapwing and, on the continent, "from the noise of its wings", *vannellus*. Elsewhere, while on the subject of the *kywit* of the Germans, he elaborates as follows: "The kywit of the Germans is, however, smaller than a crow, with the plumage almost green and black on the whole back and head and neck, the belly white, a long and always upright feathery crest upon the head, and somewhat rounded wings, which during flight make a great hurtling, whence it is even named by foreigners *Vannellus* [from the Latin *vannus* a fan]. It approaches waters for the sake of worms, on which alone it feeds, but does not enter them. It mostly lives in open country, and in places overgrown with heather. Our people often keep this bird in gardens, to destroy the worms."

Later English writers confirm the fact that lapwings were kept in gardens. Thomas Bewick (1821) describes how one kept by the Rev. J. Carlyle, vicar of Newcastle, got into the habit of entering the house in winter, calling "pee-wit" to gain entry, and took to roosting with the dog and the cat at the kitchen fireside; it even used to wash itself in the dog's bowl! In 1853 the death occurred through accident of a lapwing which had been "fourteen years in captivity, in a walled garden at Yarrow . . . in the parish of Bintry, Norfolk" (Stevenson 1870).

A page from the Emperor Frederick II's treatise *On the art of hunting with birds.*

Dr John Kay or Caius, already mentioned, who published a history of "rarer animals" in 1570 (Evans 1903), added a third plover species to the two described by Turner and therefore known in Elizabethan England—the dotterel or *morinellus*. He interpreted both names as meaning foolish, deriving the Latin name from the same Greek word that has given us "moron", and the English name from the verb to dote or doat which has given us "dotage" and "dotty". He explains that the dotterel is a foolish bird because it allows itself to be easily taken:

> "It is a mimic. And so . . . this bird is caught at night by the light of a candle according to the motion of the captor. For if he stretches out an arm, the bird lifts a wing; if he stretches out a leg, it does likewise. In short, whatever part the fowler plays, the bird does the same. So being intent on the man's actions, it is fooled by the bird-catcher and caught in his net."

Besides this quaint account of dotterel catching, Dr Caius claims that the bird makes delicate eating and he says just enough by way of description for us to be sure that his *morinellus* is our dotterel. "It is a little bird, the size of a starling [correct: the length of both is exactly 8½ inches], with only three fore-toes and no hind-toe, a black crown, white cheeks, and colour almost that of a quail, if you were to mix with it a little ash-colour, especially round the neck".

A century later, writing not long after the already mentioned Sir Thomas Browne, John Ray produced his *The ornithology of Francis Willughby*, in three books, dated London, 1678. Sir Thomas in 1662 knew the lapwing, dotterel, golden plover and ringed plover; Ray describes these species and adds the grey plover; indeed he seems to be the first British ornithologist to mention this bird, "called at Venice, Squatarola", whose winter plumage (only) he accurately describes. His "green plover" is in fact the golden plover, as can easily be ascertained by the description of the bird's plumage. But he knows little about it except that "Its flesh is sweet and tender and therefore highly esteemed, and accounted a choice dish". On the dotterel Ray quotes Dr Caius, but is not content with this. He had dissected one, and found beetles in the stomach, and he also observes that "The Males in this kind are lesser than the Females, at least they were so in those we happened to see". His account of dotterel catching in East Anglia is notable, especially in relation to Dr Caius's remarks already quoted:

> "Of the catching of Dotterels, my very good friend Mr Peter Dent, an Apothecary in Cambridge, a Person well skill'd in the History of Plants And animals, whom I consulted concerning it, wrote thus to me. A Gentleman of Norfolk, where this kind of sport is very common, told me, that to catch Dotterels six or seven persons usually go in company. When

they have found the Birds, they set their Net in an advantageous place; and each of them holding a stone in either hand get behind the Birds, and striking their stones often one against another rouse them, which are naturally very sluggish; and so by degrees coup them, and drive them into the Net. The Birds being awakened do often stretch themselves, putting out a Wing or a Leg and in imitation of them the men that drive them thrust out an Arm or a Leg for fashion sake, to comply with an old custom. But he thought that this imitation did not conduce to the taking of them, for that they seemed not to mind or regard it."

Ray is also full and interesting on the lapwing, which he points out is called "tewit" in the north of England from its call. "It lays four or five eggs, of a dirty yellow, all over painted with great black spots and stroakes"; and he mentions "as the common tradition is", that the young run away with bits of egg-shell on their heads; and also the belief "that a Lapwing, the further you are from her Nest, the more clamorous she is, and the greater coil she keeps, the nearer you are to it, the quieter she is, and less concerned she seems: That she may draw you away from the true place, and induce you to think it is where it is not". Evidently from personal observation Ray adds that "In Summer time they scatter themselves about the Country to breed. In Winter time they accompany together and fly in flocks".

Two lapwing chicks newly hatched, two eggs ready to hatch, photographed on 6th May, 1971. Usually all four young hatch within a few hours. At first the chicks' down is wet, but it dries in an hour or so. The lapwing chick is a rather dark, speckled brown fluffy ball on spindly grey legs. It has a prominent white collar. From their first moments out of the nest the chicks crouch immobile when danger threatens.

On the ringed plover, which he calls the "sea-lark", Ray is less convincing, for his account of the nest and eggs is not very accurate. He continues:

> "It runs very swiftly on the shores, and makes short flights, singing or crying continually as it flies. It is with us in England every where very common upon the Sea-coast. We also saw it about the Lake of Geneva, and it hath been brought to us killed upon the banks of the River Trent, not far from Nottingham."

It is curious that knowledge of plovers in Britain was advanced very little between the late seventeenth century and 1800. On either side of this latter year two notable ornithologies were produced — Thomas Bewick's, *A history of British Birds*, i. *History and description of Land birds,* Newcastle-upon-Tyne, in 1797, and George Montagu's *Ornithological dictionary* in 1802. Bewick has little to add about the "pee-wit" or lapwing, the golden plover, grey plover, and "ring dotterel" or ringed plover or "sea-lark;" but he does record that the dotterel was common in May and June in Lincolnshire, Cambridgeshire and Derbyshire, and bred in the Highlands. Montagu includes the same five species, rejecting the newly discovered Kentish plover as probably due to confusion with young ringed plovers. He called the grey plover the grey sandpiper — he had bought specimens in the market at Bristol. He contributes an accurate description of the ringed plover's nest and eggs, which he had himself found, and his account of the lapwing represents a notable advance on previous knowledge. For instance he points out that "It lays invariably four eggs . . ."

In the course of the nineteenth century knowledge of plovers was gradually extended. When the standard work of those days, William Yarrell's *British birds*, came out in a revised edition in 1871-1885, it was able to include full accounts of all seven accepted British plovers, namely the dotterel, the ringed plover, little ringed plover and Kentish plover, the golden and grey plovers, and the "lapwing or peewit". The last important gap in knowledge of these birds had been filled in 1876, when an account of the breeding of the grey plover on the tundras of the Petchora appeared in the journal *Ibis*. Since the mid-nineteenth century the following plover species have been added to the British list, all of them more or less rare vagrants. The dates are those on which they were added to the British list.

killdeer, *Charadrius vociferus*	April 1859
sociable plover, *Chettusia gregaria*	about 1860
lesser golden plover, *Pluvialis dominica*	November 1870
Caspian plover, *Charadrius asiaticus*	May 1890
white-tailed plover, *Chettusia leucura*	July 1975
semipalmated plover, *Charadrius semipalmatus*	autumn 1978
greater sand plover, *Charadrius leschenaultii*	December 1978

CHAPTER THREE

Plumage and Field Identification

IN THIS chapter we shall be concerned only with the seven regularly occurring British plovers—the lapwing, dotterel, golden and grey plovers, and ringed, little ringed and Kentish plovers. The field identification of the rarer visitors to Britain, among the plovers, will be discussed in Chapter Twelve.

None of the seven plovers regularly visiting the British Isles is difficult to identify in the field; nor is there much difficulty in distinguishing a plover from any other kind of bird. It is a wader, a bird of shores and open places, with a relatively short bill and not very long legs, varying in size in Britain from the pigeon-sized lapwing to the sparrow-sized little ringed plover. To put it more exactly, the approximate sizes and weights of our plovers, from the largest to smallest, are as follows:

lapwing	12 ins or 30 cm	8 oz or 227 g
grey plover golden plover	11 in or 28 cm	6-10 oz or 170-284 g
dotterel	8½ ins or 22 cm	4¼ oz or 113 g
ringed plover	7½ ins or 19 cm	2 oz or 57 g
Kentish plover	6¼ in or 16 cm	1½ oz or 42 g
little ringed plover	6 ins or 15 cm	1½ oz or 42 g

All these species have the same typical feeding habit—a run or swift walk, a pause, a jab with the bill at food on or just under the surface of the ground which is very often a worm of some kind. But they by no means frequent similar terrain, and the kind of place in which a plover is seen often helps to identify it. To summarize here very crudely the findings of our next chapter, their preferred habitats may be set out as follows:

lapwing	fields, moorland, flat sea shores
grey plover	flat sea shores
golden plover	fields in winter, moorland in summer
dotterel	fields in spring and autumn, mountain tops summer
ringed plover	flat sea shores
Kentish plover	flat sea shores
little ringed plover	gravel pits, rivers

All these plovers, in common with numerous other birds, share certain plumage characteristics. Except for the ringed and little ringed plovers, each has a brighter summer and drabber winter plumage. In each, too, except the dotterel where the reverse is true, the male's summer plumage is brighter than the female's. Finally, the juvenile in each case has a plumage more or less different from the adult's.

The moulting arrangements of the British plovers, whereby these different plumages are acquired, are all very much alike. The juvenile plumage is replaced in a partial or body moult, not involving the main wing and tail feathers, by the first winter plumage. This moult starts in July in the case of the lapwing, in August-September in the case of the other species, but perhaps not until October in the case of the grey plover. It is completed in most species by December. But individual birds may remain well into the winter in juvenile plumage, and I have even seen an apparently juvenile ringed plover as late as 22nd March. Apart from the ringed plover, all our plovers also go through a pre-nuptial or spring moult of the body feathers, thus acquiring their breeding or summer plumage; but the principal annual moult in all seven species begins immediately after breeding is over, or even sometimes immediately after egg laying, for example in the case of the golden plover. This moult has to be fitted in with autumn migration, for long-distance migrants—and all our plovers are migrants—almost never migrate without their full complement of wing feathers or primaries. Either, as in the case of golden plovers nesting in Iceland which are faced with a long oversea flight at the start of their autumn migration, the wing feathers are moulted first, in June-September, or, as is the case with a proportion of grey plovers, some primaries are moulted in late summer before the birds leave their breeding grounds, and the rest later on, in the autumn or even winter, when they reach their winter quarters (Branson and Minton 1976). Yet again, in some cases the birds repair to a special moulting area either during migration or beforehand. Thus quite large numbers of little ringed plovers assemble in the Camargue to moult after leaving their breeding grounds in late summer.

The lapwing's moult was ingeniously studied by the Snows (1976), who collected moulted wing and tail feathers from flocks of lapwings roosting in fields near their home in late summer. They found that the moult occurred between July and mid-September and they on several occasions confirmed the probability that pairs of wing feathers are moulted simultaneously and symmetrically: two feathers lying just where they had dropped during the night, one from each wing separated by a space of about a body width. Examination of birds caught for ringing has shown (Appleton and Minton, 1978) that the lapwing's moult can extend from early June to late September.

When confronted with a bird in the field which has to be identified, all the points so far discussed need to be taken into account, namely the bird's size, its surroundings, and, depending on the time of year and its age, the state of its plumage. Bearing this in mind, the following key to the field identification characters of our British plovers may be found useful:

I a Large to medium size, upright stance, slow moving on ground .... see II
b Small, body held horizontal, white neck ring, plain light brown back, fast running on ground .... see V

II a Prominent crest, back black with metallic sheen; especially in flight, a black and white bird; "peewit" call .... **lapwing**
b Predominantly brown or grey; no distinctive markings in flight ....see III

III a Rather small, white eye-stripes meeting behind head, white breast band, sometimes indistinct, yellowish legs .... **dotterel**
b Grey or yellow-brown above; underparts black or blackish in summer, white in winter; black legs .... see IV

IV a Mainly golden or yellowish upper parts; white patch on "armpit" under wing .... **golden plover**
b Mainly grey upper parts, black patch on "armpit" under wing, human-like whistling call .... **grey plover**

V a Yellowish or pinkish legs, some pink or yellow at base of otherwise dark bill .... see VI
b Bill and legs dark, outer tail feathers conspicuously white, black markings on head and neck not very prominent .... **Kentish plover**

VI a Yellowish eye-rim, dull flesh-coloured legs, wing showing plain brown in flight, very small, "pee-oo" call .... **little ringed plover**
b No pronounced eye-rim, yellow legs, wings showing prominent white bar in flight, "poo-ee" call .... **ringed plover**

Two sets of problems should confront the observer when watching or examining any bird in order to identify it: first, the question of its specific or sub-specific determination; second, the question of its status within the species—is it male or female, adult or juvenile? Our key disregards entirely the second set of problems, being designed to help with specific determination only, regardless of the sex or age of a given bird. Nor does it consider in detail, though it does try to cater for, the few cases where confusion between species is possible. It is these to which we must now turn.

The lapwing is a distinctive bird, unlikely to be confused with any of the other six species of British plover. The dotterel, too, especially in summer plumage when it has a chesnut or cinnamon-coloured breast, is fairly distinctive. But in autumn, solitary birds especially can be confused with golden plovers in spite of their smaller size; the bird must be scrutinized at rest, when the dotterel's white eye-stripe and, at closer range, white breast band and yellow legs are distinctive. In flight, neither the size difference nor the golden plover's white wing bar and the dotterel's lack of one constitute an invariably reliable character.

Golden and grey plovers usually present few identification problems; as their names imply, one is golden and the other grey. But some confusion between the juveniles in autumn is possible, especially since the juvenile grey plover does not begin moulting into its winter plumage until October and it is at first a distinctly yellowish looking bird, though much of this golden colour has faded to white by the time the birds undertake their autumn migration. Because of this, when confronted with an apparent autumn golden plover, the observer should always check that it is not a juvenile grey plover. If the bird is at rest this may be difficult, for the white rump may not be visible and the rather longer stouter bill is insufficiently different from the golden plover's. Once on the wing, however, the grey plover's white rump and more conspicuously barred tail will be apparent. The presence or absence of a white wing bar, usually indistinct, is not a helpful field character – both species have one (Bisson 1969). What is absolutely diagnostic is the grey plover's black axillary or armpit patch, usually very visible in flight, while the golden plover has white feathers in its armpit. The black axillaries also serve to distinguish the grey plover from other waders on the shore. The only one at all like it is in fact the winter-plumage knot, but this bird's longer, finer bill separates it at once from any plover.

Winter plumage of golden and grey plovers compared. The shape of the golden plover's head (left) is very different from the grey's. The grey plover (right) has a higher, steeper forehead and a flatter crown because, owing to its adaptation to salt water, it has larger nasal glands than the fresh water adapted golden plover. The grey plover is a more strongly built bird with more powerful head and neck and relatively larger and thicker legs and feet. This bird, photographed in October, is a juvenile. This characteristic spotted plumage is retained well into the bird's first winter.

The tail pattern and black axillaries are well displayed as this grey plover takes off towards the camera (above). A bathing golden plover pauses to shake its wings, revealing its white "armpit" or axillaries, and the indistinct white wing bar (right).

When we come to the three small *Charadrius* plovers, identification difficulties do arise, the more so because their differing size is of little use in the field unless two species are seen together. The Kentish plover may quickly be dismissed because the black or dark grey legs and conspicuously white outer tail feathers distinguish it from its relatives even in juvenile plumage. We should note, however, that the ringed plover which, like the Kentish plover, does have a white wing bar visible in flight but usually not when the bird is at rest, also has white on the tail, but this white is narrower and extends all round the sides and end of the tail, virtually to the tip, while in the Kentish plover, apart from the three outer feathers which are wholly white, the end of the tail is brown. The adult Kentish plover is also unlike its relatives in the small amount of black on and near its head. Throughout the year, both the ringed and little ringed plover are more or less heavily marked with black or dark brown on the head and have a black band across the upper breast. The Kentish plover, on the other hand, never has more than a small black mark across the front or top of its head, a narrow black mark through the eye and a black patch on the side of the breast. And it is only in the adult male in summer that these marks are black; in winter they are more or less brown, and the corresponding markings on the female are brown and indistinct throughout the year. The Kentish plover, in any case, is a rather rare bird in Britain, occurring regularly only in East Anglia.

A ringed plover flies past the author's hide at Spurn Head, displaying the white wing bar which distinguishes it in flight from the little ringed plover.

In spite of the size difference and the absence of the white wing bar in the little ringed plover, adult ringed and little ringed plovers need to be looked at carefully in the field to be sure of identifying them correctly. The little ringed plover is a slighter, less stocky, bird, often looking as if its body was slimmer and its tail longer than the ringed plover's. Its back appears to be a warmer shade of brown, the ringed plover's seeming greyer, stonier. As to differences in the head markings, the little ringed plover usually has a distinct white line running over the top of its head behind the black forehead band. This line is clearly visible in the photographs reproduced in this book, but it is by no means invariably visible in the field and is not therefore a very reliable field character.

Nor is the rather white appearance the little ringed plover presents when facing the observer — the white collar seems broader and there seems to be a larger white area above the beak than in the ringed plover. The little ringed plover's yellow eye-rim remains diagnostic but is only apparent at fairly close range, and the same goes for the bill colour: the basal half of the ringed plover's bill is more or less bright orange, the rest black, whereas the little ringed plover's bill is blackish except for the lightest touch of yellowish-flesh or pinkish-grey colour at the base of the lower mandible. The fact that the little ringed plover's bill is less stubby, finer and sharper, is scarcely of value in the field. Once on the wing, of course, the ringed plover's white wing bar is diagnostic, and the calls of the two species are quite distinct too.

Ringed (above) and Kentish (below) plovers compared. Both these birds, stretching out their right wings and legs in almost identical postures, are juveniles. Both have a conspicuous white wing bar which the little ringed plover lacks.

The juvenile little ringed plover above (left) may be compared with the juvenile ringed plover above (right). The ringed plover's heavier dark markings on the head and the little ringed plover's yellowish eye rim are fairly distinctive. Even so, the two are not always easy to separate in the field, unless the presence or absence of a white wing bar can be verified by the bird taking flight.

Knottiest of all the field identification problems presented by our common plovers is the separation of juvenile ringed plover from juvenile little ringed plover. Indeed, if the eye-rim is not visible and if the bird neither calls nor flies, it may not be possible to separate the two with certainty. However, the juvenile ringed plover's back appears to be somewhat greyer than the little ringed plover's. Also, the ringed plover usually has a conspicuous white eye-stripe, which is more or less entirely lacking in the juvenile little ringed plover, and the juvenile ringed plover's brownish breast-band is often more developed.

Ringed plover at nest

Migrant dotterel in Yorkshire in May

Fortunately the problem of sub-specific identification is a limited one for the British plover watcher. Neither the lapwing, the grey plover nor the dotterel has been convincingly divided into sub-species. The little ringed plover has two races besides the European one, but they are far away in India and the Philippines. The Kentish plover has several extra-European sub-species, but none are nearer Europe than the Far East, Sri Lanka or North America. Apart from the North American ringed plover, if it is a sub-species of our ringed plover, namely the semipalmated plover, so-called because of the slight amount of webbing between the toes, the solitary (pre-1978) 1916 British record of which was discredited in 1962 along with the other so-called Hastings rarities, this leaves us with the northern European races or forms of the golden and ringed plovers, both of which are common in Britain on passage in autumn and spring and probably also in winter, but neither of which is consistently distinguishable in the field. Indeed the Arctic ringed plover *Charadrius hiaticula tundrae*, though rather darker above than the ringed plover and with a darker bill, is apparently never separable in the field. On the other hand the northern golden plover *Pluvialis apricaria altifrons* has a blacker belly and more contrasty plumage in summer, and this is sufficiently distinctive for it to be evident that many of the very striking and handsome birds seen on spring migration in Britain in April and May belong to this type.

A lapwing in winter plumage photographed in November. Typically, it was feeding on worms in a grass pasture. Note the pale edges of the feathers of the back.

The difficulty here is that some authorities regard the northern golden plover as only a geographical variation, not a distinct sub-species, of the golden plover, and this indeed seems a realistic view because of the many intermediate populations (Wynne-Edwards 1957).

It remains to outline the plumage differences within each species which serve to indicate the age or sex of a plover in the field. The handsome lapwing male in breeding plumage has a long and conspicuous crest, a jet black breast sharply demarcated from the pure white lower breast and belly, black primaries contrasting with the dark greenish back, bronze shoulder-patches and bluish-green folded wings, white rump contrasting with black tail tip, and a conspicuous rufous patch under the tail. His pink legs are decorative too. At this time of year the male is easily distinguishable from the female by his blacker face and breast; the female has, in particular, more white around the eye and on the throat. She also has a shorter crest. In winter plumage the sexes are not so easy to distinguish; both are whiter about the head at that season, and have pale edges or tips to the wing coverts and scapulars, that is, the feathers on the side of the back and the upper part of the folded wing. In juvenile plumage the young lapwing is separable by its short stubby crest and very conspicuous pale edgings to the feathers of the back and folded wing, but long before the year's end most of them, now assuming their first winter plumage, have become indistinguishable from adults in winter plumage.

A juvenile lapwing photographed in August. The crest has scarcely begun to grow and the dark feathers of the back are conspicuously edged with buff as with the adult's winter plumage.

The resplendent male grey plovers in breeding plumage which one may be lucky enough to see in Britain in May or August are unmistakable. The throat, breast and belly are deep black constrasting with the pure white under tail coverts and a broad white band next to the black extending from the bill, above the eye, down the side of the neck, to the folded wing. The back and folded wing present a beautiful marbled pattern of grey, black and white. The female is at once separable by her much less purely black underparts. In winter plumage the sexes are similar: the upperparts are a rather uniform brownish grey, obscurely mottled or spotted; the underparts white, except for the grey-streaked breast. On the other hand the juveniles, whose distinctive plumage may be retained until as late as January of their first winter, have dark grey-brown backs heavily marked all over with yellow-gold or white spots (Minton 1977).

The plumage patterns of the golden plover are similar to those of the grey. In summer there is usually little difficulty in separating the male of a pair of "southern" golden plovers from the female, especially if both are seen together. The male has an indistinct black patch below the bill on the throat, a narrow indistinct black band down the throat widening on the breast to form a large blackish or black area on the belly. The female has no sign of black above the belly, and even there the black is interspersed with lighter feathers. Even in pairs where the male has very little solid black save on the lower belly, the female nearly always has even less black on the underparts and is often paler and not so brilliantly golden on the upperparts. In winter the sexes are similar and, as in the grey plover, all trace of black—except perhaps for a few black flecks on some birds—on the underparts is lost. Feeding golden plovers in winter usually show a dark mark through the eye and a light stripe above it. Autumn juveniles do not appear to be readily separable from adults.

The dotterel, a substantially smaller and paler-looking bird than the golden plover, has if anything an even more upright stance. The sexes are generally separable in summer plumage though in the case of the dotterel it is the male which is usually, perhaps invariably, the more brightly coloured bird of a pair. Typically, the breeding dotterel has a brown back, the feathers with buff edges, dark brown or nearly black crown, very prominent white eye-stripes meeting at the back of the neck or nape, a well defined narrow white band or bar across the breast separating the greyish brown upper breast from the chestnut lower breast which merges into black on the lower belly. The tail is bordered with white; the legs are yellowish. In the rather nondescript brown winter plumage the sexes of the dotterel are not separable, but autumn juveniles have the buff edges of their back and folded wing feathers interrupted by a dark tip.

The bold black and white head markings of the ringed plover, with its white collar above a black breast band, brown back and white underparts, are shared by male and female alike, while the brown-marked juvenile is quite distinctive. According to the *Handbook of British birds*, first winter and even first summer ringed plovers can sometimes be distinguished from fully adult birds by the buff edges of the wing coverts, which are retained from the juvenile plumage. As to distinguishing males from females in the field, this is certainly possible in the case of most pairs of ringed plovers in the summer. The female's head markings are usually less pronounced than the male's and indeed are more often brown-black or black-brown, even brown. One bird I observed closely had pure black only round each eye and on the breast band; she could be distinguished from her mate at a glance. Exactly the same is true of the very similarly marked little ringed plover: the female's "black" markings prove on close inspection to be, at least partly, only dark black-brown, and they are less extensive than the male's.

In most pairs of ringed plovers, the male and female are readily distinguishable in the field — the male is much more boldly marked with black.

The female ringed plover at nest; note that she is much less boldly marked than her mate.

This account of the plumages of plovers would be sadly incomplete without some mention of the chicks in down (Fjeldså 1977). It is two weeks before a lapwing chick's feathers begin to emerge through its down and nearly five weeks before it takes its first flight. The newly hatched plover chick remains in the nest only long enough to dry its down, which is wet when it emerges from the egg. Then it scampers off, reacts by crouching and "freezing" to human or other predators, and feeds itself. The chicks in down of our seven plover species share a similar colour pattern, namely beautifully marbled black and white upper parts and white underparts. Most have a more or less distinct white collar: conspicuous in the lapwing, ringed plover and little ringed plover, less so in the other species. Intermixed with the black and white markings on the back and top of the head are varying amounts of colour, a feint greeny-brown tinge in the ringed plover chick; a rather warmer light brown tint in the little ringed plover; light pinkish brown in the dotterel;

greyish brown in the lapwing. These minute, long-legged creatures, which look like quick-moving balls of fluff, are all beautiful, but most beautiful of all is surely the nestling golden plover. I once came across a nestful of them, inhibited from leaving the nest by a cold windy day. So they crouched there together, their heads and backs presenting a rich golden colour marbled with black, a colour which exactly matched some of the golden-yellow or greenish-yellow moorland mosses growing around them, just as the chick ringed plover's back colour seems most appropriate against a backcloth of the grey-green lichens of the Arctic.

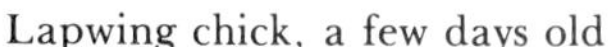

Lapwing chick, a few days old.

CHAPTER FOUR

Ecology and Food

EUROPE'S plovers are all migratory species at least to some extent, but some much more so than others. Moreover the picture is complicated further by the fact that, within any one species, some populations may be more or less migratory, others more or less sedentary. Among the European plovers we have, at one extreme, the grey plover, a long-distance migrant covering thousands of miles each autumn and spring and frequenting two quite distinct habitats: tundra in summer, the sea shore in winter. At the other extreme is the lapwing, which often frequents the same habitat in summer and winter, and some individuals of which appear to be virtually sedentary. Thus Lister (1964) found that, of 82 localities regularly checked for lapwings, 37 (45 per cent) held them in every month of the year, though almost certainly different birds were involved at different times of the year.

Let us consider, in the first place, those species with fairly straightforward, and quite different, summer and winter habitat preferences. The grey plover need not detain us long, but it should be emphasized that, although this bird—as opposed to the golden plover—is specially adapted for feeding in a salt water environment, it is by no means found exclusively by the shore outside the breeding season. Apart from mud-flats and estuaries, it may be found on sewage farms and at the margins of reservoirs and shallow grassy lakes, and it is not at all rare at such inland habitats; it is even on occasion found on dry pastures or ploughed fields. In the tundra it prefers the dryer exposed ridges and slopes, more or less vegetation free, avoiding low-lying marshy ground. The other plover with quite different summer and winter habitats is the dotterel. In summer it frequents dry stony mountain tops and, in the far north, tundra. In winter it is found on dry stony or grassy steppes, rough upland slopes and cultivated fields in semi-desert areas. On passage the dotterel often halts for a few days on moorland tops, ploughed fields, grassy steppes in eastern Europe, and other open places. Its nesting in recent years in newly-reclaimed Dutch polders will be discussed in Chapter Eight.

The golden plover frequents an extraordinary variety of habitats, especially in the breeding season. In Sweden it nests at sea level on a dry stony heath on the island of Öland called the Alvar, but it also breeds high in the Arctic fells, for example up to 1,200 metres on Svaipa, higher than the dotterel. I found a nest on the top of a hummock in the middle of a lowland bog in the Varanger Peninsula, Norway, but birds were also breeding high in the stony fells there. In England nests may be found in heather in the North Yorkshire Moors or in the grassy fells of the Pennines. The one essential requirement for breeding is a fair proportion of flat, open ground with very short vegetation, or no vegetation at all. The bird must be able to run freely and easily and see all round. Scattered bushes, even trees, or boulders, are tolerated, but a solid expanse of thick vegetation is avoided. Nests actually concealed in dense heather or other vegetation are rare and are usually on the edge of the vegetated area. In Britain the main golden plover breeding populations are on heather moor, wet heath, blanket bog, grassland and, finally, moss and lichen heath high up in the mountains, where the birds may breed side by side with dotterels (Ratcliffe 1976).

Grey plovers are seen here in a typically English winter setting, the shore of an estuary at high tide. In this case the estuary is the Humber and the place Spurn Head, Humberside. There are three grey plovers together on the extreme right of a tightly packed flock of dunlins and other waders.

It is a curious fact that much of the golden plover's breeding habitat is man-made; after all, until well into historic times large tracts of the northern British uplands were forested. Even now, many parts of this upland would be unsuitable for golden plovers because of the dense growth of heather, were it not for the clearing activities of man. Thus in the North Yorkshire Moors, parts of which support a dense breeding population of golden plovers, the heather is burned regularly because this is thought to provide more fresh shoots for sheep and grouse, and more grass. And almost all the golden plover's nests are found, not on freshly burned ground, but in areas where the heather has been burned some three to eight years previously. It is so unusual to find a nest elsewhere than on one of these burnt areas that it seems likely that, were it not for heather burning, the golden plover would not breed on the North Yorkshire Moors at all.

Another striking example of man's influence on the golden plover's breeding habitat occurred in West Germany, where much of the dwindling golden plover breeding population was for many years to be found on a low-lying heath west of the River Ems near the Dutch frontier: the Bourtanger Moor. Here rank heather growth would probably have deterred them had it not been for the centuries-old practice of the local farmers of burning the heather off in patches to plant buckwheat; then, after a few years, the buckwheat would be abandonded and the heather cleared elsewhere ready for another sowing (Steiniger 1959). Furthermore, since the Second World War, the heather has been extensively burned to promote new shoots for sheep. West Germany's breeding golden plovers linger on, but there are apparently fewer than fifty pairs remaining at the present day.

Although the golden plover virtually never nests in enclosed fields, these form an important feeding habitat during the breeding season. In some areas, at any rate, the nesting territory is little used for feeding and the birds, or off-duty bird if eggs have been laid, fly several miles to the nearest "improved" pastures to feed (Ratcliffe 1976).

In winter the golden plover leaves its moorland breeding grounds between October and February and descends to lower levels and cultivated fields (Fuller and Youngman 1979). At this season pasture is much the preferred habitat. In the recent British Trust for Ornithology golden plover survey, over 80 per cent of wintering birds in Britain were on permanent grassland. Ploughed land was used mainly for roosting; less than 5 per cent of the birds counted were on root crops, fallow ground or stubble; 7 per cent were feeding on winter cereal in eastern England. Large flocks of golden plovers were recorded, especially in the north of Britain, on the shore, either on mud flats or salt marshes—but, even so, these birds represented only 8 per cent of the total counted.

In many respects the lapwing frequents the same habitats as the golden plover. Although in summer it commonly breeds in enclosed fields while the golden plover does not, yet, in many of its moorland breeding haunts the golden plover has the lapwing for a neighbour. In the North Yorkshire Moors the very same areas where the heather has been burnt, which the golden plover uses for its nest-sites, are also used by lapwings. I have even watched a male lapwing visiting and actually scraping in a golden plover's nest scrape. In winter, too, the two species may often be seen feeding in the same fields, side by side, even though they flock separately; and the lapwing, too, often feeds on the shore and on estuarine mud-flats.

The lapwing's habitat preferences have been studied in great detail, beginning with the then quite newly-formed British Trust for Ornithology's "Lapwing Habitat Inquiry", of 1937 (Nicholson 1938 and 1939). A follow-up of this investigation, which changing editorial conventions labelled the "Lapwing habitat enquiry", was organized by the same body in 1960-1 (Lister 1964). Meanwhile on the continent H. Klomp's remarkable doctoral thesis on the lapwing's choice of terrain was published in Holland in 1953. He showed that the varying breeding densities of lapwings in different parts of South Holland were not correlated with differences in the amount of food available, but were due to their habitat preferences. In particular, long grass or high vegetation was avoided in favour of short grass or arable. He found, too, that colour was important: greyish-brown fields were preferred to green ones. Remarkably enough, when he strewed parts of a green field with cow-dung, eight pairs of lapwings settled where previously there had been none! The roughness, or unevenness, of the manured surface may have been important as well as the colour. Klomp concluded that the recent decline in lapwing breeding numbers in Holland was probably due to the change from the short grass of rather poor pastures to the taller vegetation of improved, more productive, grassland. A further significant contribution to our knowledge of this subject was made in Switzerland, where Christoph Imboden (1971a and b) pointed out that lapwing numbers had been reduced from around 500 breeding pairs before 1880 to a maximum of 150 pairs in the nineteen-thirties as a result of the drainage and reclamation of the marshes in which they formerly, and more or less exclusively, bred. But the species showed a high degree of adaptation, and a proportion of breeding pairs moved onto cultivated fields and bred there successfully, though apparently not successfully enough to account for the remarkable increase in lapwing breeding numbers since the war—to a total of about 740 pairs in Switzerland in 1970.

From just over the frontier into Austria, Imboden presented some interesting data from the large lapwing colony nesting in the delta made by the River Rhine where it flows into the southern end of the Lake of Constance or Bodensee. This colony was affected by the creation of ploughed fields from 1961 onwards after the construction of a sea wall. Though colonizing this arable land, the lapwings continued to breed on uncultivated marshy ground in the delta as well as on pastures, and it was in these habitats, and not on the arable, that the above-mentioned numerical increase made itself felt.

	1962	*1963*	*1965*	*1969*
Total number of breeding pairs:	69	132	143	about 165
Pairs breeding in marsh:		81	79	108
Pairs breeding in grass pastures:		16	17	36
Pairs breeding on arable:	1	29	41	21

The British lapwing habitat enquiries made no attempt to investigate the history of lapwing habitat preferences, but it seems likely that, as in Switzerland, so here and elsewhere in Europe, the lapwing was originally a marshland breeding bird which switched to cultivated land as the marshes were reclaimed, in Britain perhaps from the seventeenth century onwards. In 1802 (Montagu) lapwings were said to breed "upon heaths and upland situations, as well as in fens and moist fields, and not unfrequently in old fallow land". The nineteenth-century standard work by Yarrell, on the other hand, only mentioned "marshy ground near lakes and rivers, wild heaths and commons, or the hills of an open unenclosed country". In 1937 "breeding was recorded most frequently upon newly ploughed land, fair permanent pasture above alluvial level, and rushy fields", but neither the report on that enquiry, nor its successor, tried to come to any conclusion on the preferred breeding habitat. One must be content with the broad fact already well known before the lapwing habitat enquiries, that lapwings breed commonly on arable, on grass meadows, and in marshes.

On the whole, the habitats of the British *Charadrius* plovers are similar; indeed, in a notable paper published in 1954, the Dutch ornithologist J. E. Sluiters described how all three nested in identical habitats on the outskirts of Amsterdam: the little ringed plover commonly; the ringed plover more rarely; and Kentish plovers when and where a suitable habitat presented itself. This breeding habitat was man-made. It consisted of reclaimed areas of gravel, sand and clay, which had been left to dry out and consolidate ready for building or agriculture. Another man-made habitat in Holland where all three plover species nested more or less side by side was the newly-reclaimed Noordoost polder, but the growth of vegetation and the development of agriculture there caused their decline and eventual disappearance.

The Kentish plover is more often than not a bird of the coast and its most favoured habitats are sandy or shingly coastal flats or salt-pans. But it is quite prepared to nest far inland provided it can do so on the shores of a salt lake; it breeds alongside the little ringed plover in Austria's Seewinkel in the province of Burgenland, and commonly on saline flats throughout much of Asia. On the whole it prefers fine sand to stones or shingle; salt rather than fresh water.

Little ringed plover at nest on a Yorkshire colliery slag-heap.

The little ringed plover seems originally to have been a bird of shingle bars and sandbanks in rivers; certainly it is often found in conjunction with fresh water, on rivers especially, but it also breeds around saline lakes inland. It tends to eschew fine sand, preferring shingle, but it seldom nests by the sea. Indeed, apart from the Baltic, almost the only place where it nests regularly on the sea shore (as opposed to sandy flats near the coast) is on either side of the Oslo fjord in Norway, a country where it is a very local breeder and where it does also nest on fresh water. Man-made habitats have greatly contributed to the little ringed plover's spread and numerical increase since the war, for it is quick to colonize new earthworks of any kind which provide it with suitable nesting or feeding places and it seems well able to exploit temporary habitats. Thus it will nest for a year or two on a motorway or airfield construction site; it breeds commonly on slag heaps, but above all in gravel and sand pits. Indeed its spread into Britain from 1944 onwards seems to have occurred only because of the numerous gravel pits excavated in south-eastern England during and after the war.

The ringed plover, which is thought of as normally nesting on the sea shore, also breeds quite happily in many areas far from the sea. In some places it nests almost side by side with the little ringed plover, for example on stretches of some Polish rivers. But here the two species tend to choose different nest sites, the ringed plover preferring sandy pastures or hillocks near the river, while the smaller species prefers sandy or shingly river banks. Other inland habitats which are used exclusively by the ringed plover are the stony fields of the Breckland heaths in Norfolk and Suffolk and the pebbly river banks of northern Britain. An unusual habitat, where some of the photographs reproduced in this book were taken, was for a time provided by disused wartime airfields in East Yorkshire.

Plovers frequent certain habitats either for breeding or for feeding, or for both. Their feeding habits are very similar. All of them take food in the main from the surface and many of them follow the routine already mentioned of first stopping and listening, then jabbing or lunging for the food, then running or walking a short distance. Worms are often pulled out of the grass or sand, but seldom actively dug for. They seem to be located by listening.

One particular feeding habit of plovers, which has been called foot paddling or foot trembling, is of some interest. It has been observed in all our plovers except perhaps the grey (Holt 1947, Johnson 1947, Simmons 1961a and b). The function of this curious habit has not yet been fully elucidated; it is hard to believe that worms mistake the pitter-patter of the plover's foot for the pattering of rain and burrow up to the surface as a result. On the other hand the habit probably does in some way facilitate the capture of worms and other organisms.

Breeding habitats of ringed plover: above (left) on mixed sand and shingle just above the high tide line and (right) a nest in spilt coal on an abandoned airfield runway.

Foot trembling in plovers is by no means easy to see. The bird has to be observed carefully with good glasses at close range, or watched from a hide. Nor is it particularly common. I have watched golden plovers for hours and never seen it, and even lapwings, which use it relatively frequently, more often than not feed without employing it. It is thus hardly surprising that, in 1947, those three remarkably perceptive and experienced field ornithologists, the then editors of *British Birds*, Bernard Tucker, Norman Ticehurst, and A. W. Boyd, confessed that they had never seen it.

Because foot trembling is hard to see, my field notes recording observations of it are sadly incomplete. On 23rd April 1975 a female lapwing watched from a hide feeding on a soft, mossy bog in the North Yorkshire Moors—not on grass, be it noted—was seen "paddling vigorously with one foot, then bobbing forwards and vibrating her bill up and down in the peaty mud." This bird was definitely feeding but it was unclear on what exactly. On 5th March 1976 a lapwing was watched feeding and foot trembling in a grassy area in the North Yorkshire Moors. It bent one leg forwards, then jerked the foot downwards quite smartly against the ground at approximately one-second intervals, "a sort of gentle stamp" followed by a vibration, not unlike a drummer's stroke. Immediately afterwards the bird was seen on numerous occasions to tilt its body and peck a small object from the surface of the ground; an object which was seen several times to be a small pink earthworm.

A lapwing foot paddling, or trembling. One foot is moved forward, slightly raised and then stamped down against the ground.

This autumn lapwing has been caught in the act of pulling a large worm out of the ground in a newly ploughed stubble field. A Swedish ornithologist counted a lapwing's pecks and found that 23 per cent of them yielded an earthworm; in the case of the other pecks, the prey, if any, was invisible.

This bird jerked its foot down six to ten times during a stand-still, then moved on and repeated the performance. In a quite different area on 2nd March lapwings were closely watched feeding in a grass field and no foot trembling was seen throughout the afternoon; yet on 23rd March in the same field one bird was doing it most of the time—one could clearly see its leg bent forwards and rhythmically jerked against the ground every second or so, though at first glance the bird appeared to be standing still. This curious habit certainly needs to be studied further: it seems to be limited to the plovers and a few other species of wader.

A phenomenon which concerns both the ecology and the food of at least two of our plovers, the lapwing and the golden plover, is kleptoparasitism or parasitism by stealing. As long ago as 1927 Edmund Selous described how in Dorset in February he watched black-headed gulls standing among feeding lapwings on pasture land. From time to time a gull would take wing and fly at a lapwing, either settling on the spot vacated by the lapwing or chasing it some distance with loud discordant cries. He soon realized that the gull was after the lapwing's prey and that, very often, the chase ended successfully for the gull when it dropped to the ground to eat a worm dropped or disgorged by the lapwing. He noticed that, every now and then, a gull would fly up to and settle near a feeding lapwing, which would take no notice of the gull. It was as if the lapwing accepted the gull's presence and had no fear of it, and as if the gull was, as it were, reminding the lapwing of its duties. Selous remarked on the fact that only certain individual gulls preyed on the lapwings;many others were following the plough in a nearby field, ignoring the lapwings, and those that did practise this piracy on the lapwings did nothing else.

As a matter of fact the Swedish ornithologist Hans Källander (1977) recently calculated that a gull preying on lapwings' worms could subsist, at any rate for a time, on this source of food alone. Those he watched succeeded in obtaining one earthworm about very four to five minutes. He also thought that the gulls maintained a kind of mobile territorial system which caused them to be more or less dispersed among the lapwings, with two to six lapwings per gull. This kleptoparasitism has also been recorded of the common gull, and golden plovers as often as lapwings seem to be the victims of it. These two species frequently feed together and on two separate occasions I have observed lapwings chasing golden plovers and apparently successfully stealing worms from them in just the same way as do the gulls. Again here, more observations are required.

Any account of the actual food found in plovers' stomachs, as opposed to their feeding habits, is liable to become a dry catalogue of Latin names of more or less obscure organisms. It could also be somewhat misleading, concealing the fact, for example, that the staple diet of both the lapwing and golden plover, throughout a large part of the year, is very probably the common earthworm, *Lumbricus* species. In lists of stomach contents earthworms are invariably under-represented, for this soft prey soon disintegrates, leaving hard fragments of insects to predominate.

In winter the ringed plover becomes quite gregarious and forms into flocks, usually mixed with dunlins. Photographed below is part of such a mixed winter flock. The birds are feeding with two dunlins, on the sand at low tide at the South Landing, Flamborough, apparently on small worms. Because of the wind, they are all facing in the same direction.

The lapwing's diet in Britain appears to have been seriously investigated only once, by W. E. Collinge in 1924-7. He analysed the stomach-contents of 69 birds, and found 89 per cent animal and 10 per cent vegetable matter. Of the animal matter, he calculated that worms comprised a mere 10 per cent, molluscs 10 per cent and "injurious insects" 60 per cent. Among the insects, moths and their larvae and beetles figured largely. In fact, the lapwing probably picks up and eats everything edible that it comes across, including slugs, spiders, grasshoppers, and even small frogs, fishes and bivalves; above all, however, it subsists on worms and beetles (details in Glutz von Blotzheim).

Like the lapwing, the golden plover does eat a certain amount of vegetable matter, much of it grass; the *Handbook* (Witherby) gives a figure of 23 per cent vegetable matter, based on 17 stomachs. All the main groups of insects and other small animals living in or on the soil or in grassland are represented in the golden plover's diet: earthworms, slugs, snails, moths and their larvae, beetles, dipterous flies, ants and spiders. On the sea shore they obtain small crabs, bivalves and other molluscs, and various worms.

The grey plover's food is not very well known. Like the golden plover it certainly supplements its animal diet with vegetable matter; in late summer and autumn in particular with berries of the bilberry and crowberry. Like the golden plover too, it takes beetles and other small organisms, but its predilection for the shore means that marine worms, molluscs and crustacea are more often taken; it has been watched feeding on cockles and one has been seen with a mussel firmly clamped to its bill (Hori 1962). In summer on its

The actions of golden plovers feeding in winter on worms are very similar to those of the grey plover. The golden plover pulls worms out of the soil very much as the grey plover pulls them out of the mud. A golden plover (right) leans forward in an almost crouching position with its head stretched forward and the bill downward-pointing. It is "listening" for a worm — a moment later this bird made a quick jab at the ground and pulled one out.

breeding grounds it has been found to feed on beetle grubs and caterpillars as well as many different insects.

The dotterel's diet does not seem to differ very much from that of the golden plover, though it may take fewer earthworms. It has been seen feeding on craneflies, spiders and houseflies, and beetle fragments and earthworm remains are a feature of its stomach contents; wireworms, larvae of various kinds, and small snails have also been recorded among its prey.

The ringed plover's diet depends on its habitat but is formed either by small beetles and other insects, or by marine worms and molluscs. Besides Diptera (two-winged flies) and Coleoptera (beetles), Lepidoptera (butterflies and moths) and Hymenoptera (ants, bees etc) are taken and, on the shore, periwinkles and mussels seem to be favoured, along with the nereid worms. As one would expect, the little ringed plover takes more water beetles and other fresh water organisms, larvae especially of dipterious flies, spiders, annelid worms, crustacea and some vegetable matter. As for the Kentish plover, its diet consists of small nereid worms, mussels, periwinkles, small crabs and other small marine organisms.

A grey plover with a worm. Not very much has been scientifically ascertained so far about the diet of this species, but this worm is almost certainly the ragworm *Nereis diversicolor*. This identification is confirmed by the fact that the grey plover was feeding on the Humber mud and only two animals live at all commonly in this mud, the worm and a crustacean.

CHAPTER FIVE

The Kentish Plover

IT IS most unfortunate that the inappropriate name "Kentish" for this plover has been retained by English ornithologists and bird-watchers even though it has long since ceased to breed in Kent. The Kentish plover was first described in Britain by the ornithologist John Latham, who received specimens in 1787 and 1791 from Sandwich in Kent, sent to him by a certain Dr Boys. When he included this species in a supplement to his *General synopsis of birds*, naming it *Charadrius cantianus*, he was quite unaware of the fact that it was the species already described by the Swedish naturalist Linnaeus in 1758, and named, since Linnaeus based his description on specimens from Egypt, *Charadrius alexandrinus*.

During much of the nineteenth century the Kentish plover was an extremely local but regular breeding bird at a handful of coastal localities in Kent, notably around Sandwich and Pegwell Bay between Ramsgate and Deal, at Dungeness, where it is said to have been plentiful in the mid-nineteenth century between Dungeness and Littlestone (Alexander 1974), and possibly in East Sussex as well. Nests were plundered and the adult birds shot by collectors, but these small colonies persisted, and, even in the 1870s and 1880s, it was thought that some fifteen pairs were still breeding in Kent (Bannerman 1961). In about 1890 an egg collector took three clutches at Shellness in Sandwich Bay, and in 1898 the Kearton brothers located three pairs on shingle flats near the Channel coast, presumably Dungeness, and found a nest containing three eggs (Kearton 1899). An increase in breeding numbers seems to have taken place at the turn of the century, especially on Dungeness, where, after a decline to about fifteen pairs around 1900, twenty-one pairs reared young in 1905, the first year of really systematic protection there. In 1906-8 between thirty and forty-five pairs bred on these immense shingle flats, but thereafter numbers dwindled until in the 1930s breeding was only sporadic (Alexander 1974). The decline has been attributed to commercial development. Just when pressures from egg collectors and collectors of skins relaxed and protection began to be effective, bungalows and roads were being constructed, and the birds themselves were being increasingly disturbed while their favourite habitats were thus destroyed. The Hythe to Dungeness light railway passed right through the centre of the main colony. But the railway was built before the Kentish plover disappeared and the bungalows afterwards; perhaps it was the egg collectors after all, or climatic changes, which sealed its fate in Britain.

At the start of the twentieth century the Kentish plover was found breeding at Humberston on the north-east Lincolnshire coast. Actually this is far too euphemistic a way of putting it: in fact a nest was robbed and a clutch of eggs taken on 1st June 1903 which still exists in the City and County Museum at Lincoln. Three other clutches are said to have been taken in the same locality between 1902 and 1905 (Smith and Cornwallis 1955). The Kentish plover is supposed to have bred at Shellness in Sandwich Bay, Kent, in 1932-5 and at Rye Harbour in East Sussex between 1949 and 1955 or 1956. In 1952 a nest containing three eggs was found at Walberswick in Suffolk, but the eggs disappeared shortly before they were due to hatch. This, so far as published records are concerned, seems to be the end of the history of the Kentish plover as a breeding bird in the British Isles, except for the Channel Islands, where a few pairs still breed annually. As a passage migrant, however, the Kentish plover is still a British bird, for a few turn up every spring and autumn, usually on the south or east coast. Norfolk is the preferred county and April-May and August-September the favourite months.

In the nineteen seventies there have even been some signs of an increase in Kentish plover numbers, and the possibility arises that it may once again breed here. In Norfolk, for example, the pattern of the sixties was a very few, sometimes (1969 and 1970) only one (in 1958 none), each year. A record year at that time was 1964, with seven occurrences in the county. But from 1973 onwards a new pattern, of repeated occurrences in April-May and again in August-September, has become established; and pairs have appeared in early summer and remained together for days at a time at favoured localities like Cley, Blakeney, Breydon and Winterton.

The extinction of the Kentish plover in Britain, which was always on the fringe of its range, has scarcely had any impact on the status of the species as a whole, though the decline in the numbers breeding here may well have been a symptom, or a result, either of a general decline in numbers, or of a shrinking of the range of the species, or of both. The Kentish plover is much more widely distributed throughout the world than either of its British *Charadrius* relatives, for it breeds in North and South America, Europe, Asia and Australia. In Eurasia the main axis of its range lies approximately along the Tropic of Cancer, while that of the little ringed plover lies to the north, along the forty-fifth parallel, and the ringed plover's range is even more northerly, lying roughly speaking along the Polar Circle.

Ornithologists have divided the world population of Kentish plovers into twelve or thirteen sub-species, giving the largest area, namely the whole of Eurasia—China and Japan apart—and the North African coast, to our

European race *Charadrius alexandrinus alexandrinus*. The American population falls naturally into three discrete groups—those in the West Indies and the coast of the Gulf of Mexico; California and the North American west coast; and the west coast of South America in southern Peru and Chile. The birds breeding in Africa, which extend along both east and west coasts but not round the Cape of Good Hope, and comprise also some important inland populations, have been assigned to at least four more sub-species, and there are a further two or three races in the Far East and Australasia. Sri Lanka has its own sub-species of Kentish plover.

As one would expect from what has been said about its world range, the Kentish plover is a more common breeding bird in southern Europe than in the north. In Norway it was found nesting in the 1880s south of Stavanger but there has been no evidence of breeding since 1888 and there are only a handful of records, of passage birds, from Norway since then (Haftorn 1971). In Sweden a few pairs breed in the extreme south of the country at Skanör or along the shore of the Öland and Öresund (Rosenberg 1967). Up to about 1948 the species also bred, occasionally at least, on Öland. Further south the story is similar, namely one of decline. In the Netherlands, although it was thought in the early 1970s that there were over 1,000 pairs in all, numbers were declining; the population breeding on the island of Texel dwindled from 35 pairs in 1965 to half-a-dozen pairs ten years later. In Belgium, where in the last two decades there have been more than 100 breeding pairs in any one year, the species has diminished in number in the coastal dunes. For example at Knokke, where some 70 pairs nested in 1945, there were only about 25 pairs in 1970. But coastal losses, which in Belgium as elsewhere have been due in the main to the development of tourism, have been partly compensated for by temporary increases where major earthworks have been carried out. At Zeebrugge, where a single pair of Kentish plovers bred in 1957, there were 35 in 1968 (Lippens and Wille 1972). There is no doubt that the Kentish plover has declined in France, where the *Atlas* (Yeatman 1976) estimated a grand total in the early 1970s of fewer than 1,000 pairs, less than 200 of which were in Brittany. In 1936 it had been described as a common breeding bird; forty years later it had become rare—there were thought to have been only about four breeding pairs between Boulogne and Calais, for example.

In the German Federal Republic the Kentish plover breeds in the East Frisian Islands, where some 130 pairs nested in 1971, the North Frisian Islands and coast of Schleswig-Holstein, with about 600 pairs in the early 1970s, and various other places (Glutz von Blotzheim 1975). Again here, there has been a marked decline and a tendency for the birds to colonize coastal man-made earthworks. When Rittinghaus (1961) studied this species on the Frisian Island of Oldeoog in the 1950s there was a breeding population of up to nearly 100 pairs; in 1970 there were only 14 pairs, in 1973 only 6.

A Kentish plover feeding in a Spanish salt-pan.

As in the general area of the North Sea and Atlantic coasts of north-western Europe, so in its few inland European breeding stations, the Kentish plover population has recently suffered a severe decline. At the eastern end of Austria, in the province of Burgenland, some 60-80 pairs were breeding in 1944 in the area of shallow lakes known as the Seewinkel, east of the Neusiedler See. By the 1970s this number had been reduced to 35-40 pairs. A similar reduction has occurred in the Hungarian plain south of Budapest—the only other area in Europe where Kentish plovers breed inland.

The shores of the Mediterranean and Black Seas constitute the European stronghold of the Kentish plover and there is no evidence here of the decline in numbers so apparent in the north of its breeding range. Thus it is still a common bird in suitable flat sandy coastal areas, especially where there are salt-pans, in Spain, the Balearic Islands and Italy. Except in the Canary and Cape Verde Islands, Tunisia and parts of the Arabian Peninsula, where it is apparently resident throughout the year, the European sub-species of the Kentish plover is a summer migrant, arriving on its breeding grounds mainly in March-April, or May in the north, and departing in August or September. It winters in south Spain, the Balearic Islands, Sardinia, southern Italy, Sicily, Greece, southern Turkey and northern India, and southwards from these areas as far as the Gulf of Guinea, Nigeria, the Gulf of Aden and Sri Lanka. Ringing, supported by field observations, has shown that the Kentish plovers breeding in the North Sea and Baltic area migrate almost exclusively in autumn along the Atlantic coasts of France, Spain and Portugal. Inland records are rare at this time of year. Assemblies, apparently of moulting birds, occur in early autumn in the Wattenmeer off the Danish and North Frisian coasts, in the Delta area of the Netherlands, in the Bay of Biscay, and in the Camargue. The local breeders from this last area mostly migrate south-west via the Spanish coast or across Spain to Morocco, but some move south through Italy. Ringed Hungarian breeders have been recovered in Italy, showing a similarly predominant south-westerly autumn migration. The return migration in spring is often more direct, and overland flights are frequently undertaken: apparently the birds are then in a hurry to get "home".

As has been pointed out in the chapter on field identification, the Kentish plover may not always be easy to distinguish in the field from the ringed and little ringed plovers, especially when juveniles are concerned. But its calls are quite different from those of its relatives. The usual call is a "pit" or "tit", often repeated, sometimes to the extent of forming a trill, and used especially before and after flight. This is frequently the first sign the observer has of the presence of Kentish plovers along the shore ahead of him as these tiny birds race across the sand. When excited, the Kentish plover calls "huit" or "weit"; when alarmed the call has been rendered "prrr". Other notes are less often used. The male's song flight, during which it patrols its territory with a butterfly-like flight, is accompanied by a repeated "rrai-jai-jai-ai", as written down by a German ornithologist; and a rapidly repeated "tjekke-tjekke-tjekke" is also uttered. It seems that the Kentish plover's song flight is less often heard than those of related species. In all his years of study of these birds on the island of Oldeoog, Rittinghaus never once observed it.

Nevertheless, in spite of this one lacuna, Rittinghaus's observations on the Kentish plover, which were brought together in his book *Der Seeregenpfeifer* (1961), form the basis of our knowledge of the breeding biology and general behaviour of this species. One of the most easterly of the East Frisian Islands, Oldeoog, lying between Wangerooge and Mellum, is only two or three acres in extent, yet in the nineteen-fifties, the years of Rittinghaus's studies there, up to 96 pairs of Kentish plovers were nesting. Over a period of thirteen years Rittinghaus ringed 481 adult birds and 1,590 juveniles there. He was able to trace the life histories of individual birds and even to work out their family trees. Some of them returned to Oldeoog up to nine years in succession, either returning in their first summer to breed there, where they had emerged from the egg the year before, or turning up in a subsequent year or years after apparently breeding elsewhere in the intervening summer or summers. Often a male returned to the same territory, or patch of sand, and even nested in virtually the same spot, in successive years. One ringed male nested every year between 1948 and 1954 within a circle about 16 metres across. His mate was the same individual in 1948 and 1949; in 1952-4 he had three different mates; but in 1955 he reverted to his mate of 1952.

Rittinghaus's Kentish plovers returned to Oldeoog in groups or singly in late March or early April. Some were paired on arrival, but most pairs were formed thereafter. Once two Kentish plovers have paired and established themselves in a territory the male begins making scrapes in the sand, in one of which the female will eventually lay her eggs. Nests are lined or adorned with small stones, shell fragments, or pieces of dead grass, but this lining is simply the result of the bird picking objects up off the ground with its beak and throwing them over its shoulder as it leaves the scrape or nest. As with other plovers, both sexes engage in nest scraping, the male, however, taking the lead, and courtship display and copulation are closely associated with the scraping activities. Once an egg is laid, the scrape becomes a nest.

Unlike its relatives, the Kentish plover lays only three eggs, never four. Though nests containing four have been recorded, they are almost certainly due to two females laying in the same nest. J. Walters found only two four-egg clutches among 389 nests near Amsterdam. Munn, in Majorca, came across one four-egg clutch among 290 nests found; and Rittinghaus never recorded four eggs in a nest. He made a careful study of egg-laying by a number of females on Oldeoog and found that the three-egg clutch was completed in from four to seven days; that a forty-eight hour interval normally separated the laying of each egg; and that eggs might be laid at any time of day. Incubation often started immediately after the third egg had been laid but early nesters, which laid in April, sometimes delayed the start of incubation for up to three days.

Incubation is divided between the sexes. At three nests of twelve watched by Rittinghaus through the day, the male incubated for between 50 and 60 per cent of the time; in another three it incubated for less than 25 per cent of the time; and in the other six it incubated for between a half and a quarter of the

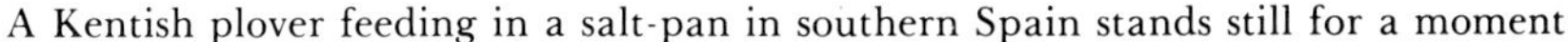
A Kentish plover feeding in a salt-pan in southern Spain stands still for a moment.

time. But the male apparently incubates in the evening and perhaps usually also at night; if this is so, his total share of incubation may be more than half. Meinertzhagen's belief that, at any rate in Africa, the Kentish plover sometimes covers its eggs with sand on a hot day to protect them from the sun, has yet to be confirmed for Europe; so has its reported habit from India, of wetting its eggs (Crossley 1964). Rittinghaus thought that eggs sometimes got covered with sand on hot days because the bird sat less tightly then so that sand blew in over the eggs. Incubation lasts for between twenty-four and twenty-eight days.

Shortly before the eggs hatch the parent Kentish plover's behaviour changes abruptly and it reacts to disturbance at the nest by injury feigning rather than merely by taking flight and calling anxiously. This injury feigning continues after the young have hatched. How do the adults "know" that one of their eggs is about to hatch? Presumably they can hear or feel the young bird pecking at the inside of the shell; certainly too they must be able to hear its high pitched cheeping, which begins some fifty hours or so before the hatch.

Once the newly hatched chicks are dry, that is within two or three hours of hatching, they leave the nest and begin to run about the territory. They have to find their own food, but for a time they are brooded at night and in wet weather by one or other of their parents. The parent birds also warn them of danger and distract the attention of potential predators or enemies by the injury feigning already mentioned. In the case of the Kentish plover this may take the rather unusual form of an adult bird crouching stationary on the sand with tail lifted up and both wings held open or partly open and often raised somewhat in the air. The Kentish plover also uses the so-called rodent run, in which it creeps along the ground with depressed tail and one wing trailing. Adult Kentish plovers also play an important role in leading or guiding their young, in particular keeping them together and within the territory. Thirty or forty days after hatching the young birds fly.

The breeding success of the Kentish plover has been investigated by several observers. Rittinghaus found that, of 168 eggs belonging to 56 nests, 158 hatched; but this probably represents a substantially better than average result. On the neighbouring island of Wangerooge about 20 per cent of the eggs failed to produce young for one reason or another. In 1955 90 per cent of first clutches failed but replacement clutches did unusually well. For Belgium, an average figure of one and a half to two flying young per pair has been estimated. Elsewhere, two hatched eggs and one and a half flying young per pair seems about the norm. Young Kentish plovers are particularly vulnerable to predators, especially gulls, and to bad weather. Various calculations based on ringing and recovery data point to an annual adult mortality rate among Kentish plovers of about 40 per cent. The oldest recorded Kentish plover lived for thirteen years.

CHAPTER SIX

The Ringed Plover

MOST modern authorities now regard the long-billed ringed plover or Ussuri sand plover *Charadrius placidus* of eastern Asia, and the North American semipalmated or webfooted ringed plover *Charadrius semipalmatus*, as distinct species, though both are in many respects very similar to the ringed plover, and their ranges on the whole do not overlap with that of the ringed plover. The ringed plover, breeding from Baffin Island – where it does overlap slightly with the semipalmated plover (Smith 1969) – eastwards right round the Arctic to the Anadyr territory in the far north-east of the Soviet Union, has been divided into two races or sub-species which are, however, exceedingly ill-defined: *Charadrius hiaticula hiaticula* of Greenland, Iceland, the Faroes, Spitsbergen, Scandinavia, the North and Baltic Seas and the British Isles; and *Charadrius h. tundrae*, which is smaller and darker, of the Russian-Siberian tundra. Some authorities (Prater *et al.* 1977) on the other hand, ascribe the northern Fenno-Scandinavian population to *Ch. h. tundrae.* Still others, sensibly, are loth to accept division into sub-species, preferring to talk of two clines, both starting in the south-western part of the range, one reaching north-westwards to Greenland, the other north-eastwards to Siberia (Vaurie 1964).

The ringed plover was perhaps originally an Arctic bird, breeding all round the North Pole. Later, brought southwards by successive ice ages, it became in southerly areas either a coastal breeding bird or a bird of sandy or gravelly rivers, nesting sometimes far inland. In Europe it is essentially a bird of the north-western Atlantic coastal fringe. On the other hand in northern Russia and Siberia it is widespread on the tundra but apparently prefers to nest within sight of water – either the sea, a river, or a lake. As an inland breeder, mainly along rivers, it is commonest in Iceland, in Scotland and parts of Ireland, in southern Scandinavia and in Poland. Quite exceptional was the discovery of 11th May 1952 in south-western Bohemia, Czechoslovakia, of a breeding pair of ringed plovers with a clutch of four eggs.

The ringed plover may occasionally breed in the Mediterranean area, especially Spain, but there are few substantiated records; perhaps the most acceptable are those of a nest in Majorca in 1929 and one near Fos in Provence in 1958. In France the ringed plover was first discovered breeding in 1941 on an island off the coast of Brittany; now it is thought that there are between 10 and 100 pairs in all, some 60 of them in the Molène archipelago in Brittany—the only locality where breeding is regular. In Belgium it is a very local breeder—the harbour earthworks at Antwerp and the nature reserve of the Zwin at Knokke are among the few more or less regular breeding sites, but even so it is only a question of the odd pair. Even in Holland the ringed plover is not at all a common breeding bird; there may be some 150 to 200 pairs in three main areas: the West Frisian Islands—Texel had 32 pairs in 1974—the Ijsselmeer and the area between the Wieringermeer and Den Helder, and the "Delta area" in the south. Moving northwards and eastwards into West Germany, we find the ringed plover a much commoner bird; for example some 600 pairs nest on the North Frisian island of Sylt. On the other hand East Germany and Poland together only have some 400 pairs, mostly along the Baltic coast. In Scandinavia, however, the ringed plover is common and widespread, and the same applies to Iceland, the Faroe Islands and Greenland. On the north-east coast of Greenland it is said to be the commonest breeding bird, and it nests both on the coast and along the river valleys all round Greenland except in the extreme north-west between Peary Land and Inglefield Land (Salomonsen 1967).

The *Atlas of breeding birds in Britain and Ireland* (Sharrock 1976) provided the first detailed description, in map form, of the ringed plover's breeding distribution in the British Isles. It claimed that over 90 per cent of ringed plovers breed on the coast and that 70 per cent of these coastal breeding birds nest on sandy, shingle or shell beaches. It also pointed out that there was an increasing tendency to breed inland, especially in northern Britain, where the shingle banks of rivers and the shores of lakes are favoured. In the south, power station or oil refinery compounds, farmland near sea walls, and gravel and sand pits were the principal inland sites. While these were being increasingly occupied, the once flourishing breeding population of the East Anglian Breckland, which could be numbered in hundreds of pairs earlier in the century, dwindled to a few pairs, a decline brought about in the first place by forestry, perhaps also by land reclamation for farming, and subsequently greatly accelerated by the decimation of the rabbit population by myxomatosis, which allowed rank grass and heather to grow in former areas of sandy waste.

The *Atlas* map shows the ringed plover to be distributed rather evenly and quite thickly round the coasts of Britain. It is however rare or local in Devon and Cornwall, Dyfed, Cork and along much of the coast of North Humberside and North Yorkshire. The scarcity in the first two areas is perhaps explicable in terms of the fact that Britain and Ireland are near the extreme south-western point of the ringed plover's breeding range; the other areas mentioned have limited amounts of suitable habitat—for example the Yorkshire coast is mostly cliff. The map shows that the ringed plover's main breeding areas in Britain are the north and west of Scotland, including especially the Orkneys and Shetland and the Inner Hebrides, western Ireland, Lancashire, Cumbria and East Anglia.

In 1973 the British Trust for Ornithology made a brave attempt to estimate the size of the breeding population of ringed plovers in Britain by counting as many pairs holding territories in April-June as possible, and by extrapolating from *Atlas* data in areas where counting was impossible because of a shortage of observers (Prater 1976). Unfortunately, no details were published of the degree of coverage nor of the census methods, so that its accuracy cannot easily be assessed. We are told, for example, that "in 1973-74 the number of pairs of Ringed Plovers breeding in England was 1,878" and in "Wales, 186. . ."; but we are not told to which of these two breeding seasons these astonishingly exact figures apply. And our faith in them can only be further shaken when we read elsewhere that "The results obtained from England and Wales form an almost complete picture," implying that other pairs may have existed which are not included in the figures. The slap-dash methods of some modern so-called censuses — for this survey is actually called a census — are revealed by the figures for Northern Ireland. The numbers of pairs actually mentioned in the report add up to 90-92; yet we are told in one place that the "estimated total of Ringed Plovers breeding in Northern Ireland is at least 93 pairs" and in another that "the number of pairs of Ringed Plovers breeding in Northern Ireland was . . . c. 93". Surely a round figure of 90-100 would be more informative if less apparently accurate? The final figures, which apparently vary from a fairly accurate count for parts of England (margin of error around 10 per cent?) to mere guesses for parts of Scotland, may be compared with some tentative estimates of numbers of pairs in certain continental European countries (Glutz von Blotzheim 1975):

Area	Pairs
England, 1973-4	1,878
Wales, 1973-4	186
Isle of Man, 1973-4	c.75
Northern Ireland, 1973-4	c.93
Scotland, 1973-4	c.3,565
Total for Britain, sum of above figures	5,797
Total for Britain stated elsewhere in the report on the 1973-4 survey	5,800-6,300
Poland, 1973	260-285
East Germany, 1972-3	c.120
Schleswig-Holstein, West Germany, 1970	c.1,100-1,200

Approximate numbers of breeding pairs of ringed plovers in certain areas, 1970-4.

The adult ringed plover develops an aggressive hostility towards its offspring once they have become independent. This male bird, seen here in full threat display aimed at a juvenile bird, invariably chased away any juveniles which invaded its territory; the time was early September, the place north Norfolk.

It has been stated that "the Ringed Plover breeding population has shown quite a dramatic decline in S. England during the last 50 or so years" (Prater 1973). If this is true, as seems likely, and if the ringed plover has declined seriously elsewhere, this must surely be largely because of human disturbance. Pressure on the coast nowadays is such that many of the denser concentrations of ringed plovers occur within protected areas or nature reserves. Elsewhere, breeding sites are invaded, disturbed, even obliterated. Worrying, too, is the evidence of the British Trust for Ornithology's Nest Record Cards. These reveal (Sharrock 1976) that many of the nests discovered by human beings never hatch: some 60 per cent are predated by gulls, crows, foxes, rats or other mammals; about 17 per cent are washed away by high tides; and the rest are destroyed, accidentally or otherwise, by man. They have also been said to show (Prater 1973) that ringed plovers nesting in southern England now have "smaller clutches and a lower hatching rate" than twenty years ago, and that in eastern England only about 12 per cent of clutches hatch successfully. Thereafter, a considerable mortality must occur among chicks. Even in less disturbed areas, only about one in three clutches hatch successfully. On the other hand a 1930 study by Marples of over forty nests gave a hatching success rate of 92 per cent. According to Boyd (1962) the ringed plover's average adult annual mortality rate is around 42 per cent, and he cited a study which concluded that only about a third of eggs laid hatched and that less than half the young hatched flew. According to Laven (1940), who studied ringed plovers in a much disturbed part of the Courland Spit, each breeding pair produces, on average, only one young each year. More conservation measures are urgently required along our coast, and efforts need to be made to protect ringed plovers which have taken to nesting in gravel pits and similar sites.

Most of our breeding ringed plovers seem to remain in this country in winter, though moving south-westwards to some extent. A few move as far as the Atlantic coasts of France and Spain. The British Trust for Ornithology's Birds of Estuaries Enquiry has shown that, in December-February, around 9,000 ringed plovers are to be found in British estuaries, and it seems reasonable to assume that most of these are British breeding or British bred birds, though ringing has shown that birds from southern Scandinavia and Germany also winter here. Their ranks are swollen greatly from April onwards by passage birds moving north. The mean number of ringed plovers in Britain in May is claimed to be only a little under 20,000 birds, and, after a drop in summer, this number is surpassed during the autumn peak, when an average of 27,335 birds are said to have been counted.

The British estuary or inlet that regularly holds the highest number of waders is Morecambe Bay. In winter only a minute proportion—less than 2 per cent—of the national total of ringed plovers is to be found there, but in early autumn the figure rises to 7-8 per cent; and in May to over 35 per cent. It has been shown that most of the Morecambe Bay ringed plovers on passage in May are birds heading for Greenland. These northward-bound birds tend to remain for a short time only, during which they put on fat in readiness for the flight to their breeding grounds, which is apparently thereafter accomplished virtually without a halt (Clapham 1978).

While British breeding ringed plovers tend to be short distance migrants only, those breeding in the far north move much further south than the British birds. Thus the Greenland-breeding population winters in Africa, including tropical Africa, and Scandinavian and German breeders tend to winter on the Atlantic coasts of the Iberian Peninsula, though some remain as far north as southern Britain. The situation is complicated by the fact that some Russian and Siberian-breeding birds, belonging to the so-called sub-species *tundrae*, that is Arctic ringed plovers, move south-westwards in autumn to winter in the Mediterranean and North-west Africa; many others, probably the bulk of them, migrate south of the Sahara as far as South Africa.

The ringed plover has a quite varied repertoire of calls, the most frequently heard being the one also used as an alarm note, "poo-eep" or some variant of it, including a briefer "tuit". The call used to accompany the aggressive or threat display, when the bird runs forward with head lowered, back feathers raised, and tail fanned and depressed, has been somewhat inadequately described as "a rather liquid and fast 'toodle-toodle-toodle'" (Simmons 1953) and elsewhere, rather better, as an excited "tee-lew, tee-lew, tee-lew", "the calls getting more and more rapid until they sounded like a continuous 't'lew, t'lew, t'lew, t'lew, t'lew'" (Edwards *et al* 1947). The authors of the *Handbuch der Vögel Mitteleuropas*, basing their description on Laven (1940), render it in German "tehüe—tehüe . . . tehüt . . . hüt . . . hüt" and they rightly add that the intervals between what is often a quite prolonged series of notes, declining in complexity and intensity, are very brief. An adult bird I watched one year on several successive days early in September repeatedly directed this display at juvenile ringed plovers that approached it, running at them with hunched posture for 30 to 50 yards and driving them off, sometimes causing them to fly. I wrote down its rapidly repeated note as "er-weev-er-ter" or "tu-weeveter" (p. 58 above).

Special calls are used by the ringed plover while nest scrapes are being made, that accompanying the nest scraping action itself being a repeated tri-syllabic "pi-pi-pi". The male calls continuously while carrying out his zig-zag song flight over the territory "quoy quoy quoy" or "te-wee-er te-wee-er te-wee-er" or even "wee-per-ter wee-per-ter wee-per-ter"—the last being similar if not identical to the note used during the aggressive display already described. A soft "quip quip" is used at the nest during incubation when one bird relieves the other. Finally, when on the subject of a bird's calls, one should not forget the very high-pitched "cheep" of the chick inside the egg; Laven recorded a ringed plover calling in its egg-shell for two days before it hatched.

To this day much of our detailed knowledge of the ringed plover's breeding biology is due to the remarkable pioneering study of the German ornithologist H. Laven of the Königsberg Zoological Institute. He worked on the hundred-kilometre long strip of shingle and sand called the Courland Spit (Kurische Nehrung), then in East Prussia and now in Lithuania, part of the Soviet Union. He marked many of the breeding ringed plovers with coloured rings along a twelve-kilometre stretch of the spit. In 1936 he had a pair under observation which laid four successive clutches, each of four eggs, beginning in the third week of April (2 eggs on 25th April) and ending in the first week of July, when the fourth clutch was laid. The first three were robbed by crows or humans. He found several examples of the same two birds forming a pair in successive seasons; when this happened the nests were, on average, about 500 metres apart. Of 68 chicks ringed by Laven, only five or six returned in a subsequent year, and only two of these bred in his study area. On the other hand he found that the adult birds nearly always returned to their breeding area, many to the same territory, year after year. One year old birds were frequently found breeding, and their plumage seemed to be no different to that of older birds, being just as boldly marked with black.

Ringed plovers settle on their breeding grounds in March or thereabouts. Like other plovers, they tend to nest in straggling colonies and to hold small territories round the nest in which they do not exclusively feed. Thus in 1944 at Malahide, near Dublin, Mason (1947) found two adjacent ringed plover territories, measuring respectively 35 × 25 yards and 35 × 30 yards. The birds fed mostly on the neighbouring saltmarsh, which was evidently extra-territorial, in a loose flock. Sometimes territories are smaller than this. On 27th May 1961 at Holme in Norfolk I found five ringed plover's nests on a single sandy spit: two were within 10 yards of each other; another two were only 7 yards apart. Nearby was an extensive saltmarsh where the birds could feed.

Although near neighbours, this pair of ringed plovers reacted strongly whenever the oystercatcher approached near their eggs on its way to its own nest. The sitting ringed plover would leave the eggs and both birds would stand near the oystercatcher calling anxiously, and when it turned away, they followed it. The two nests were twelve feet apart.

Mason found that the ringed plover, unlike small passerine, or perching, birds, which only hold territories against their own species, drove off birds of all species which entered its territory. I once found a ringed plover's nest within about 4 metres of an oystercatcher's nest. In order to ascertain what was their relationship, I moved a hide into a position equidistant between the two nests and settled down to watch what happened. As far as I could gather, the oystercatcher was entirely oblivious of the ringed plovers, less than half her size. But the ringed plovers had clearly not become used to the near presence of the oystercatcher. Although the nests themselves were not all that close together, the oystercatcher's normal route back to her eggs took her quite close to the plover's nest, and it was when she was on her way back to her eggs, walking slowly and deliberately, then standing stock still for some moments while she persuaded herself that the coast was clear, that the oystercatcher really bothered the ringed plovers. On these occasions the male ringed plover would run anxiously forwards towards the intruding oystercatcher. At the same time he would utter the "poo-eep" note, calling his mate off the nest to join him. Then, together, the two ringed plovers would, so to speak, escort the oystercatcher off their territory. The degree of agitation of the ringed plovers varied according to the proximity of the oystercatcher to their nest. If she passed some distance away, one ringed plover would escort her, without troubling to call its mate off the eggs and without making a fuss. But if the oystercatcher approached the nest closely, one of the ringed plovers would dart at it with the threat display or even feign injury in front of it, or else it would indulge in another distraction display, bowing its breast to the ground as if hollowing out a nest-scrape in the sand, calling "whip-whip-whip". These manoeuvres were ignored by the oystercatcher, who resumed her stately walk up to her nest. Once she was safely brooding her eggs, the ringed plover returned to its nest and all was soon quiet on the beach.

The ringed plover's breeding behaviour starts at the end of March or early in April as soon as territories have been taken up. In 1970, in what is now North Humberside, I found a nest containing a single egg on 6th April. I watched the owner walking about nearby, apparently at random, picking up wisps of grass and small stones here and there with its bill and throwing them over its "shoulder". That day and the next the male's song flight round and over his territory was often seen. It was an erratic zig-zag, the bird dipping sometimes almost to the ground and calling repeatedly "too-wee-er". Once I was lucky enough to see the pair copulating, an event which is preceded by the extraordinary "marking time" display of the male, who draws himself up to his full height and raises one leg right up straight in front of him, then the other, while approaching the female. This is done slowly and deliberately: he towers over her, presenting his white breast to her, then mounts, remaining for some time on her back. The close of copulation is marked by the male raising his wings and grabbing the female by the neck feathers with his bill. Then he descends and both birds walk away with hunched backs to preen or at least go through the motions of preening.

To see the ringed plover's courtship and nest-making long hours of patient observation are required. I have watched a pair in the early spring for three or four hours continuously and seen nothing. Watching a pair for the best part of a day, I found that, once every 1-3 hours, the male bird visited his four nest scrapes, which were within a circle of approximately 100 yards in diameter. He walked or ran from one scrape to another, the female following. Some scrapes had small stones round their rims, or in them; others were empty. The male would sometimes merely stand briefly at a scrape; or he might settle into it and scrape vigorously with his feet, the tail being held up in the air. On such occasions the female would approach right up to him and he would get up and fan his tail feathers while she settled into the scrape to take her turn at the work.

The photographs below were taken on a disused airfield, where a colony of ringed plovers has established itself since the war. Shown here are the preliminaries to copulation. The male stretches himself to his full height, fluffing out his white breast and appearing to stand on tiptoe as he approaches the somewhat hunched female (left). While doing this he marks time slowly with a kind of goose step. First one leg is raised high, then the other (right).

Ringed plovers copulating. The male has just mounted onto the female's back and is about to seize her neck feathers with his bill. Copulation usually takes place near one or other of the scrapes.

These ringed plovers, and others which I watched in 1970-3, were nesting on a disused airfield near Bridlington. For seventeen years since the last plane took off the runway had been left abandoned, and the rotting, gravelly, often mossy, tarmac became an ideal breeding place for ringed plovers, only a few miles from the sea. Ideal for watching too, for one could drive one's car anywhere one liked and watch the ringed plovers in comfort from this mobile hide, which they mostly ignored completely. In May 1971 I spent several afternoons photographing a pair with a nest on a slight earthy mound near the edge of the old airfield runway. They were so tame that I eventually found myself photographing the incubating bird from the car window, exactly 12 feet from the nest! The male was bolder and tamer than the female. At first he left the nest when I put my hand out of the car window; later he sat on even when I waved a handkerchief out of it, only leaving when I opened the door and got out! The first time I waved a handkerchief he left the nest and feigned injury, running away in a crouching posture, holding his body sideways and lowering one wing. When some distance away he lay down on the tarmac on his side and moved along dragging his tail and one wing (compare Williamson 1947).

On several occasions I watched the behaviour of a pair of ringed plovers during incubation. On 12th June one year the two birds alternated at a nest as follows:

1000 hours.	I arrive in car; female leaves nest, male returns and incubates for 1 hour 40 minutes
1140	Female incubates until 1225 (40 minutes)
1225-40	Male incubates for 15 minutes
1240-1332	Female incubates until 1332 (52 minutes)
1332-52	Male incubates for 10 minutes
1352-1501	Female incubates (69 minutes)
1501-12	Male incubates for 11 minutes
1512-1542	Female incubates for 30 minutes
1542-1603	Male incubates for 21 minutes
1603-1700	Female incubates and was still sitting when I left

Share of incubation of male and female ringed plover during a seven-hour period

At this nest both birds incubated but the female took the main share of the work; other observations seem to confirm that the female ringed plover incubates at least twice as much as the male. The changeover only once entailed both birds being at the nest together; usually one left when the other was six to ten yards away. Both birds called "quip quip" or "pip pip" during nest relief and the male sometimes picked up stones in his bill and threw them over his shoulder, as during scraping. At other nests the male invariably picked up stones in this way as he left the nest. Aggressive display aimed at intruders was seen when a pheasant, or another male ringed plover, approached near the nest.

At another nest the incubating female was seen to run off the eggs twice when a crow flew over, and again when a rook settled near. It would be interesting to know if this behaviour is common; the eggs probably are a good deal better camouflaged than the sitting bird, whose movement away from them would in any case distract the predator from the nest itself.

On 14th May 1971 I arrived at a ringed plover's nest within hours of the hatch. The oldest chick was running well over the tarmac, using its tiny "wings" to right itself after its frequent tumbles. It had run as far as 60 yards away from the nest, while the youngest could scarcely even walk and seemed to be still rather wet. Both parent ringed plovers were attending the three chicks, but only the female was seen to brood them—which she did some 30 yards from the empty nest. Both the adult birds repeatedly feigned injury, but only some distance away, flapping along the runway dragging the spread tail making a quite loud rasping noise with their wings against the ground. The next morning the chicks were running about strongly up to 150 or 200 yards from the nest. The male brooded one chick for a time; later each adult was seen to brood one of the two smaller chicks, but the female brooded much more readily than the male.

This pair of ringed plovers was photographed in the early morning of 7th April, 1971, at their nest scrape, which is between the two birds. The bird on the left is the male. He leaves the scrape, in which he had been sitting, as the female approaches, and displays briefly with body held horizontal, tail slightly depressed and somewhat fanned, and wings held partly open (above). Then he picks up a small stone (below) in his bill which he will drop over his shoulder so that it falls into or near the scrape. Throughout the time she is close to her mate, the female ringed plover adopts a characteristic hunched posture.

A female ringed plover in characteristic attitude broods her chicks on a disused airfield runway. Ringed plovers brood their chicks at night for some time after the hatch; these are less than twenty-four hours old.

A Swedish observer (Regnell 1965) has contributed some accurate details of the incubation and fledging periods of the ringed plover. He found that at least 24 hours elapsed between the laying of each egg, and that the incubation period was about 24 or 25 days. Young birds took at least 33, and perhaps as many as 38, days to fledge. Other observers have recorded 48 hour intervals between some eggs of a clutch; and the fledging period has been stated to be as short as 21 to 23 days. The ringed plovers appears to be double-brooded in some parts of its range and single-brooded in others. Replacement clutches are the rule.

No discussion of the ringed plover would be complete without some reference to the remarkable, but unfortunately only very preliminary and provisional, study by George Marples published in *British Birds* in 1931. He carried out a number of experiments at several of more than forty nests he had under observation in May 1930. The first of his egg retrieval experiments was not a success; the cock bird simply pecked at an egg Marples had placed six inches away from the edge of the nest, and then ignored it. He continues:

> "The same experiment was tried at Nest 19, which also had four eggs. Here an egg was placed three inches away only. Almost at once one of the birds returned and dragged the egg into the nest. Two eggs were now placed outside, each at a distance of three inches. These were replaced immediately the parent returned. Next, one egg was placed six inches outside; this also was retrieved as soon as its owner came back. Each time the bird which returned to the nest was the hen, and on no occasion did she peck the eggs as they lay outside. The method she adopted to retrieve

the eggs was the same each time. She first sat on the nest, then, going to the outside egg, placed her chin over it, pressed it to her breast, and holding it in this position backed towards the nest, dragging the egg with her. A similar performance took place at Nest 32. Here the nest was on a slope, and the egg might have been dislodged from the nest by some injudicious movement of the bird, and rolled to the spot, six inches away, in which I placed it. At once the male came back, and standing between the egg and the nest, looked first at one, then at the other, puzzled. He decided to sit on the nest, but while there was uneasy, until, getting up, he went to the egg, which he took between his chin and breast, backed up the little hill, and so returned the egg to the nest. Next on one side of the nest an egg was placed at a distance of nine inches, and on the opposite side another, three inches away. It was the hen which returned this time. She sat on the nest, shuffled about, turned, then, seeing the nearest egg, she went to it, and using the same method as the other birds, brought it back to the nest. She brooded her three eggs for a while, then suddenly caught sight of the fourth egg. Stretching out her neck, she considered it for a while, went to it, and with chin and breast backed it into the nest. Nest 29 was among stones similar in size to the eggs. Here all four eggs were placed outside, three being three inches, and one six inches away. The hen came back and went on to the empty nest. She soon sensed that something was wrong. Then she caught sight of an egg, which she at once pulled in, shuffling and brooding it. She soon brought in another egg, but still a little agitated, got off, walked about a little, then back to the nest, from which she at once rose and fetched in a third egg. After that she seemed satisfied, ceased to call, and settled down, leaving the remaining egg unretrieved. The three eggs were again placed outside, this time six inches away, the fourth being placed in a hole from which a stone was removed, at a distance of nine inches from the nest. When the bird returned, she stood some yards away, then going to one of the eggs and standing over it as if to brood, extended breast-feathers to enclose it, but did not actually sit down. She now ran to the empty nest, and settled herself there as though the eggs were beneath her, but not for long. Calling gently, she left the nest and ran about. Returning, she brooded another outside egg, then leaving it, settled down on her still empty nest, uneasily moving. Next, she got off and fetched in one of the eggs, sat for a moment and kicked strongly, making small stones fly out behind. Rising, she went to the egg in the hole, pulled at it, but failed to get it out, so went back. In a moment she was off again, going to another of the nearer eggs, over which she put her chin, and ran backwards, dragging it into her nest. She was still worried, turning round in the nest and shuffling, looking now and then under her breast-feathers as though to count the eggs, jerking her head up and quietly calling. She now sat for some time rather more contentedly, brooding the two eggs she had rescued, seemingly not thinking of the other two. After some time I placed all four eggs just outside the nest. Running back at once, she sat on the empty nest, and put out her breast-feathers to enclose the eggs which were not there. Finding nothing to brood she ran some half dozen yards, then back, and at once pulled in three eggs, quickly, one after the other, tucking each one under her breast-feathers. She again nestled down comfortably, to all appearance oblivious of the fourth egg. Presently I put her off the nest. Returning at once, she retrieved the fourth egg and settled herself low down in the nest, not to be disturbed again from incubation until her chicks appeared on May 26th."*

Certainly, then, the ringed plover could retrieve displaced eggs, and Marples had no difficulty in ascertaining that it could also excavate its eggs when they were covered by sand. Years later the Dutch worker Walters (1956) showed that the same went for the Kentish and little ringed plovers. But how does the ringed plover recognize its eggs? Marples's experiments with false eggs made of wax or stone and painted like a ringed plover's egg, showed that weight was not important, nor apparently were the markings on the egg, not even the colour. Real ringed plover's eggs, painted to resemble as closely as possible the surrounding stones, and placed near the nests, were ignored. On the other hand eggs painted yellow, blue and red respectively, and placed outside nests, were retrieved, the yellow one quickly, the other two after an interval. Dark grey stones painted to look like ringed plover's eggs were readily adopted, but when the paint was washed off they were ignored. Eggs whose shape was altered with plasticine were accepted by the birds. Marples concluded that eggs were recognized by their general tone and that the ringed plover was probably colour blind. Other experiments showed that it had no sense of smell, and, since additional eggs to a total of six were adopted, the ringed plover is apparently unable to count.

Some of Marples's experiments may be regarded as suspect, and all of them need following up. His suggestion that the birds preferred to have their eggs aligned on the cardinal points of the compass is hard to accept, though at some individual nests birds repeatedly replaced their clutches in this way after he had disarranged the eggs. This work on clutch rotation and the rotation of individual eggs leaves a good deal to be desired. Although Marples found that the eggs were normally moved around by the birds, in some clutches the eggs were always arranged in exactly the same way. Thus at one nest, number 17, visited on six consecutive days, in which the eggs were numbered one to three and the fourth left unnumbered, they were always arranged with egg no. 1 facing north, egg no. 2 west, egg no. 3 south and the fourth unmarked egg facing east—just as Marples had placed them on the first day.

*Excerpt by kind permission of the editors of *British Birds*.

CHAPTER SEVEN

The Little Ringed Plover

IN EUROPE the little ringed plover is a summer migrant, wintering for the most part south of the Sahara, though north of the Equator. A few winter in the Mediterranean area and round the coast of the Arabian Peninsula. The breeding range, which stretches right across Asia to the Far East, lies in the main to the south of the ringed plover's range.

The little ringed plover breeds in England and Scotland, southern Norway, Sweden and Finland. In the west it is fairly widespread in France, especially along major rivers like the Loire, Durance, Rhine and upper Rhône, in some areas on the coast, sometimes alongside the Kentish plover, and in gravel and sand pits; but it breeds only sporadically in Spain. The southern limit of the breeding range extends to North Africa in Morocco, Algeria and Tunisia, and the little ringed plover apparently breeds on most large Mediterranean islands, as it does throughout inland and central Europe. Nowhere especially common, it tends to breed in loose colonies of up to 10 or 12 pairs where suitable habitats are available: for example, 14 pairs were found breeding on a single spoil heap in Hamburg of about 3.5 hectares (7 acres) in extent. Along rivers with sand or gravel banks and islands breeding density reaches one pair per kilometre of suitable river.

West Germany seems to be the European headquarters, as it were, of the little ringed plover. The authors of the *Handbuch der Vögel Mitteleuropas* recorded the following estimated total number of pairs in 1968-1973 in the different Länder:

Schleswig-Holstein	150-200
Hamburg	at least 60
Niedersachsen	at least 500
Nordrhein-Westfalen	at least 500
Hessen	165
Rheinland-Pfalz	50
Saarland	4-10
Baden-Württemberg	c.130
Bayern	250
Total of these figures	1,809-1,865

Apart from Britain, where over 400 pairs were said to have nested in 1972 (Sharrock 1976), other countries are less well documented. The French *Atlas* (Yeatman 1976) listed the little ringed plover as "not numerous" and estimated the total number of breeding pairs to be between 1,000 and 10,000: the actual total must be much nearer the first of these figures. Some detailed counts from Poland suggest that there must be at least 350 pairs breeding in that country, mainly along rivers; and there are over 650 in East Germany. In the Netherlands there are perhaps 200 or more breeding pairs; in Belgium 150-175 pairs were estimated in 1969; but in Switzerland there were thought to be only about 15 pairs in 1971-3.

The total population of little ringed plovers in Europe is thought to have fluctuated considerably in recent times. At least two influences have been at work: climatic change and human activity. The former caused a marked diminution in numbers in the late nineteenth and early twentieth centuries, for between about 1880 and 1920 the climate of Central Europe at least and probably also that of most of the rest of Europe, became more maritime and less continental. The cold wet summers of this period, with the high water levels and dense vegetation they promoted, did not suit the little ringed plover. Moreover this time of deteriorating climate coincided with increased interference by man in the traditional river-bed breeding habitat of the little ringed plover: one after another new stretches of river were regulated and controlled for the benefit of shipping and water conservation and the shingle banks beloved of these birds were eliminated.

The climate of much of Europe improved again from the early 1930s, becoming more continental, and the warmer drier summers, especially of the late forties and early fifties, greatly favoured the little ringed plover, which now began to extend its breeding range in many areas. And this spread and increase in numbers was facilitated by the rapidly increasing provision of suitable new "artificial" breeding habitats by man; not only gravel and sand pits proliferated everywhere, but also motorway and other construction sites, industrial sites of various kinds, and land reclamation schemes. As early as the 1930s pairs of little ringed plovers were reported breeding on autobahn clearances in Germany (Dathe 1953). But this colonization of man-made habitats was slow to begin in other areas, for example in Switzerland it has really only occurred in the last ten years.

Many English writers have implied a contrast in habitat preference between English little ringed plovers breeding in gravel and sand pits, and continental birds breeding along river beds and banks (Simmons 1953, even Sharrock 1976). In fact under 10 per cent of continental birds now nest in the original riverine habitat and, by the time the little ringed plover began to nest in Britain, the colonization of man-made habitats on the continent was in full swing.

Little ringed plover pair at a slag heap nest; the male is on the left.

The first pair of little ringed plovers to nest in Britain was discovered in 1938 on the dried-up stony bed of one of the reservoirs near Tring in Hertfordshire (Ledlie and Pedlar 1938). Up to that time the little ringed plover had been recorded in Britain only about a dozen times. Thereafter up to three individuals were noted on passage in southern England almost annually, until in 1944 three pairs were found breeding, two at Tring, one of them "in exactly the same locality as in 1938" (England *et al.* 1944), and the third in a gravel pit "in the Ashford district of Middlesex". In spite of repeated attentions paid to them by numerous ornithologists, which included the photography of one pair at the nest, these three pairs of little ringed plovers succeeded in producing a probable total of nine flying young from twelve eggs.

From then on the birds never looked back. In the following summer they were seen at four gravel pit sites, and nesting was proved at two Middlesex gravel pits; in 1946 at least four pairs summered in Middlesex; and in 1947 a quite startling extension of both range and numbers took place. "Six pairs were located in Middlesex, single pairs bred in Kent and Berkshire, and no less than four pairs were found breeding on the gravelly bed of the William Girling reservoir under construction near Chingford in Essex" (Parrinder in Bannerman 1961). The first nesting in Suffolk and Yorkshire took place in 1948, and in Sussex and Buckinghamshire in 1949.

In 1964 Parrinder estimated the annual rate of increase of the little ringed plover in Britain to have been about 15 per cent. Pointing out that between 1959 and 1962 the rate of increase in southern England was 13 per cent as opposed to 30 per cent in the north, he suggested that the difference could have been due to a more sustained immigration from the continent in the north than in the south; or more plausibly, to the greater activity and enthusiasm of northern birdwatchers in searching for breeding pairs of little ringed plovers in an area where they were newcomers, while in the south they were already well established.

Parrinder (1964) showed that the breeding range of the little ringed plover in Britain coincided quite exactly with the region of gravel extraction. He also pointed out that there was no shortage of suitable habitat: of the 90 individual little ringed plover breeding sites recorded in 1962, some 60 or 70 were gravel pits; yet some 1,400 pits were being worked in 1960. Only one report had come to hand at that time of nesting on a shingle river bed—on the River Trent in Derbyshire in 1950. Unfortunately, he was unable to report such favourable breeding success statistics as those of the three 1944 pairs already mentioned; quite the contrary. Though quantitative data were sadly incomplete, it was clear that breeding success was severely limited by flooding or wet weather, by lorries, excavators or workmen, by filling with soil or rubbish tipping, by suspected robbery of nests by collectors or children, and by predators. Parrinder cited the case of 17 clutches in Essex in 1955 laid by 9 pairs of little ringed plovers: only 8 of these clutches hatched and probably fewer than 20 young flew. One of these pairs nested four times, each unsuccessfully. In 1962, of 4 Huntingdonshire pairs which laid at least 7 clutches in all, only 7 chicks hatched and only three of them fledged.

In a later paper, the Parrinders (1969) dealt with the little ringed plover in Britain in 1963-67. At the end of this period about 230 pairs were nesting in Britain but the annual rate of increase had declined to around 8 per cent. On the other hand both in 1964 and 1965 two pairs were found nesting on river shingle in Yorkshire. Of the 154 separate sites occupied in 1967, 108 were gravel pits, sand pits or quarries of some kind, three were reservoirs, four were sewage farms, two were disused airfields, 16 were waste ground and industrial dumps, and 14 were areas associated with coal mining.

A male little ringed plover performs its spring song flight over a Humberside gravel pit. The bird flies round its territory, intermittently gliding on fixed wings, inclined first on one side and then on the other, while calling "a cree-ah a cree-ah" and occasionally trilling loudly.

The voice of the little ringed plover has been described in detail by Simmons (1955). He listed the various notes as follows:

1. The alarm note, the most frequently heard call, "an incisive, whistling 'pee-*u*'; or, when young are present, a repeated "pee-pee-pee-pee-pee *pee-u*".
2. The alarm or threat note, heard from breeding adults only, "a rather fluty, short and clipped 'cru'", also rendered "prip".
3. The general threat note, used during aggressive behaviour and threat display, a ringing musical trill "gree-gree-greegreegreegree." This call is also used by the male during his territory-patrolling song flight.
4. The aerial threat note is a development of the general threat note used only in the air by the male bird during the flight-threat display. It is "a peculiar, mechanical buzzing, very fast and continuous". It is often heard during the male's song flight when he approaches and "buzzes" intruders.
5. The song note, uttered by the male, "a slow, deliberate and rusty 'cree-ah(k)-cree-ah(k)-cree-ah(k)'. . .". This is rendered by Sluiters (1938) "griä griä griä". It is repeated at intervals of about a second and may be kept up for five or ten minutes more or less continuously. Walters (1957) studied the male's song flight near Amsterdam in 1954-56 and found that there were 13-15 calls every 10 seconds. When the birds passes close a preliminary note, before the "cree-ah". becomes distinctly audible, so that the song would be more accurately rendered "a-cree-er, a-cree-er, a-cree-er".
6. Simmons's scrape ceremony note can only be effectively heard by watching the birds from a hide at very close quarters. The male has a varied and extensive vocabulary while he is in the nest scrape, much of which is also apparently used by the female when she takes her turn there. Prominent is a repeated "wee-er chip, wee-er chip," also "chip chip chip"; the "wee-er" element in the first of these may be the same as Parrinder's "kwee-voo, kwee-voo", mentioned by Simmons.
7. The distraction display note is not often heard, and then only during "very intense distraction-display". It is "a peculiar combination of two sounds . . .: a fast, relatively high-pitched, nasal chatter . . . with a rather squealing tone super imposed" (Simmons 1955).
8. The parents' call-up note is a rapidly-repeated "pip-pip-pip" used to re-assemble the chicks after their dispersal by an intruder.
9. The small chicks' location call is a high-pitched cheeping made by the chick to announce its location to the parent.
10. The alarm note of the chick when handled is a "rather high-pitched, purring trill".

As Simmons himself admits, these ten calls certainly do not represent the little ringed plover's complete vocabulary. I have heard a throaty "crruup" call from a female approaching a nest to relieve an incubating male. Both sexes also used a repeated "coy-eeper" or "quee-ber" note at the nest which is apparently the "quoyp, quoyp" of some observers.

Simmons (1956) also studied territory in the little ringed plover. He found that single males often arrive in spring before the females. Each pair of plovers very soon adopts a particular quite restricted area in which they spend most of their time; outside these areas are "neutral" non-territorial feeding areas.

The territory is patrolled by the singing male and "defended" against other little ringed plovers and also against ringed plovers and Kentish plovers. But the male little ringed plover will attack many other birds while it is patrolling its territory. The territory is apparently used primarily for reproductive behaviour and nesting, but many birds feed in their territories if food happens to be available there. The chicks may be led away from the territory to the "neutral" feeding areas, or they may remain in the territory. Wherever they are, they will be "defended" by their parents, instead of the territory. Simmons concludes that the most important function of territory in the little ringed plovers is probably to space out the nests, for this, in conjunction with the cryptic colouration of the eggs, must make it harder for predators to find them.

Near the scrape, the male little ringed plover repeatedly picks up small stones with his beak and throws them over his shoulder. All our breeding plovers do this, the ringed plovers with small stones, the lapwing and golden plover with twigs or pieces of grass.

Not very much has been added to our knowledge of the breeding behaviour of the little ringed plover since the detailed studies of Sluiters near Amsterdam (1938), Hugo Wyss of Basel (1946) along the Rhine, and Dathe (1953) and Stein (1958) in Germany, and the already-mentioned work of the English plover enthusiast K.E.L. Simmons, partly summarized in 1953. In Germany, birds arrive on their breeding grounds in mid-March. Pairs are soon

Golden plover incubating. North Yorkshire Moors

Male little ringed plover on nest

Lapwing incubating

When the male little ringed plover (above and below on right) is at the scrape and the female approaches he leaves it and, flattening his body in the horizontal plane, he depresses his head, holds out his wings somewhat and fans his patterned, white-tipped tail while straightening his legs.

formed, territories taken up, and the males are soon patrolling their territories with their butterfly-like song flight and busying themselves making scrapes, one of which will subsequently receive the eggs and become a nest. When scraping, the male uses one of the special calls already described, and his conspicuous black and white tail, held up in a flagging movement, may attract, and is probably designed to attract, the female's attention. Certainly she often approaches, usually coyly, a few paces at a time; pretends to feed, then again advances. Eventually she arrives at the scrape. As she approaches the male, he get up out of the scrape, arches his back, spreads his wings and tail, and bends forward in a horizontal but somewhat hunched posture. While she begins scraping in her turn, he starts picking up small stones with his bill. These scraping ceremonies increase in intensity and duration until they reach a climax when the first egg is laid. On 2nd May 1975, at a Humberside breeding site, I was lucky to be in a hide near the scrape when this event occurred; the egg was actually laid between 1015 and 1130 hours and both birds were present at or near the scrape during most of that time. After 1130 the male disappeared, but the female returned several times to her single egg and picked up stones and threw them over her shoulder each time as she left.

The male little ringed plover (left, both photographs) is here displaying in response to the female's presence. The female is seen scraping vigorously, sometimes with tail up, sometimes down, in the nest scrape. Very soon after these photographs were taken she laid her first egg in this scrape.

The pre-copulatory display of the little ringed plover is very similar to that of the ringed plover. The male edges towards the female, puffing out his feathers. He seems to be prancing, his whole body shivering, vibrating. He puffs and struts; one leg is suddenly raised up high in front of him then brought down again. His lovely white breast looks whiter than ever, and his size seems to be increased by the puffed out feathers. But he does not stretch himself up so tall as does the ringed plover in similar circumstances. Eventually he mounts the female or, if she rejects his advances, will run off with crouched gait to the nearest scrape and begin scraping.

On three occasions I have seen a male little ringed plover, immediately after apparently being rejected by the female in those circumstances, throw himself into a sort of fit, for a very brief moment, fluttering his wings and shaking himself in a flurry as if momentarily crazed, becoming totally disorientated so that he appears to fall over and indeed actually does fall over. This curious behaviour is not at all like a normal plumage shake which all birds indulge in from time to time, especially while bathing.

The little ringed plover's eggs are smaller than the ringed plover's but very similar in general appearance, although they are perhaps more finely speckled and the spots browner and less black. A single egg, when fresh, weighs about 7.4 grams on average. Since an adult bird weighs some 40 or 45 grams, a full clutch of four eggs weighs about two-thirds the weight of an adult bird. Compare this with the white stork, whose normal four-egg clutch weighs only 13 per cent of an adult stork's weight. No wonder the little ringed plover often lays its eggs at two-day intervals. Laying dates vary from year to year: at a Humberside site a full clutch of four eggs was found one year on 24th April and in the following year another was found on 27th April. On the continent eggs are often found in the first half of April.

A curious case of a mixed clutch of ringed and little ringed plover's eggs was recorded from the north-east tip of Gotland, which forms a separate island called Farö, in the Baltic. On 9th June 1937 S. Durango (1943) found a nest containing a single little ringed plover's egg. On the following day he found that a ringed plover had laid an egg in the same nest. He inspected it on successive days and recorded the following:

11th June	2 little ringed plover's eggs, 1 ringed plover's egg
12th June	2 little ringed plover's eggs, 2 ringed plover's eggs
13th June	the same
14th June	2 little ringed plover's eggs, 3 ringed plover's eggs
15th June	2 little ringed plover's eggs, 4 ringed plover's eggs

Unfortunately we are given no further information about this nest except that apparently the ringed plovers remained in possession of it. A similar mixed clutch had previously been recorded, also from Sweden, and also containing four ringed plover's and two little ringed plover's eggs. A third example was found in an Essex gravel pit in 1968 (Parrinder 1969), containing four little ringed plover's and three ringed plover's eggs. On 15th June a little ringed plover was incubating this clutch; on 17th June a ringed plover had taken possession in spite of attacks by the little ringed plovers, and on 29th June the ringed plover was still incubating, but the nest then contained only four eggs, three of ringed and one of little ringed plover.

Incubation with the little ringed plover begins with the third or fourth egg and continues for 22-28 days; the average length of incubation being given by J. Walters as 24.9 days. The temperature of the eggs is maintained at about 40-42 degrees C. and incubation is shared by both sexes more or less equally, the birds changing over at intervals of from 5 to 130 minutes—longer at night, shortest in the middle of the day. If a clutch of eggs is lost the birds will normally re-lay; Wyss noted a pair which began a replacement clutch in the first half of May within six days of losing their first clutch.

The little ringed plover's eggs begin to cheep and crack several days before hatching. When they hatch, the fragments of egg-shell are carried away from the nest by the adult birds, which either fly off or run away from the nest with the shell fragments in their beaks; sometimes they eat them. The newly hatched little ringed plover chick must be one of the smallest wader nestlings; it weighs a mere 5 grams (as against the Kentish plover chick's 6 grams, Walters 1961), but its big long legs enable it to leave the nest within hours of hatching. The parents, each of which seems to take an equal share in brooding and caring for the chicks, lead them away from the nest on the day of the hatch. The chicks have to find their own food from the start, but on very hot days the parents have been watched carrying water to them by wading in a pool up to their bellies and then flying at once to them. The first feathers start appearing about 7 days after hatching and it is three weeks before even the most precocious little ringed plover chick takes its first flight. It is not easy to measure the fledging period accurately and be sure that the premature attempts at flight are not due to human disturbance, but all the evidence points to a normal fledging period of 21-29 days, with 24-26 days as perhaps the most usual.

The distraction display of the little ringed plover, which is similar to that of the ringed and Kentish plover, has been described by E. A. Armstrong (1952). This behaviour is usually seen only when chicks are present, and it is much rarer in this species than in the ringed plover (Rosenberg and Nielsen 1957). Armstrong recognized three main elements in it. The crouch-run, when the bird runs away squatting; the squat, when the bird freezes and remains quite still on the ground; and injury simulation, when one wing is flicked or raised in the air, then the other, always at a distance of at least 25 yards from the observer. During injury feigning, especially, the bird exposes its white plumage and the black-and-white tail pattern.

A curious fact which many observers have noted when watching breeding little ringed plovers is the frequent presence of a third bird alongside the breeding pair. But it is more than merely alongside; it is so attached to the breeding pair that it seems to act as a sort of "friend of the family" (Hölzinger 1975). This "friend of the family" is a non-breeding little ringed plover at least a year old; it must not be confused with the fledged young of the breeding pair's earlier brood. It has been seen helping to defend the territory, taking turns with incubation, caring for the young and assisting in defence against enemies. There is even some evidence that the "friend of the family" shares in the breeding pair's sex-life. Some of the observations made on one of the pairs breeding at Tring in 1944 are interesting in this context (England *et al.* 1944):

> "It is deserving of note that although we have not absolute proof, there is strong suspicion that three birds, two hens and one cock, were present all the time . . . an odd bird was seen by several observers at some distance at a time when both cock and hen were known to be near the nest. On the day when one bird was brooding three young and the other incubating one egg, the incubating bird suddenly flew behind the hide and started calls which were quite new to me (a variant on the Little Tern chatter). I groped for a hole behind me and found one just in time to see the finish of coition between two birds. This cannot be taken as absolute proof, as it is just possible that in the moment when I was groping for a hole the bird brooding young flew round behind me (she was back on them when I turned round again). If so, coition occurs after young have hatched—if not, the cock was practising bigamy."

Is the little ringed plover double-brooded? It certainly lays replacement clutches, but in my limited experience in eastern England and Yorkshire, second broods are certainly not the rule. Indeed I have no proof of them ever being produced. It seems that, throughout the northern part of the breeding range, second broods are rare. Further south, in southern Germany for example, they are more frequent, but even here they seem to be dependent on the weather and on an early start to the first brood. It would be interesting to know how many really well authenticated cases there are of two broods in England; one suspects very few indeed. After all, it is not an easy thing to prove in any case.

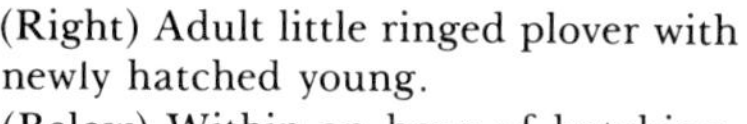

(Right) Adult little ringed plover with newly hatched young.
(Below) Within an hour of hatching, the young little ringed plovers have left the nest and begun to venture off on their relatively well-developed sturdy legs. While the adult broods the other chicks, one is off on its own.

According to Boyd (1962) the death-rate of the little ringed plover can be calculated as 35 per cent plus or minus 10 per cent; another figure is 45 per cent. Boyd gives figures of 2.22 or 1.55 as the average number of young fledged by each English breeding pair, and points out that an adult death-rate of 35 per cent requires an output of 2.13 fledged young per pair to maintain a stable population. At Amsterdam, Walters found that, of 35 hatched chicks, only 11 to 12 actually fledged, giving a fledging success rate of 31-34 per cent of eggs hatched. Hölzinger and Schilhansel (1972) recorded near Ulm in Germany that 77.7 per cent of eggs laid hatched, and that about half the chicks hatched flew. In general, hatching success seems to be about 50-60 per cent of all eggs laid, but only 25.5 per cent of over 800 eggs laid near Amsterdam hatched. The overall breeding success has been put at 36 per cent. That is, 36 per cent of eggs laid produce fledged young. The oldest recorded little ringed plover was a still breeding female which had attained the ripe old age of eleven years.

CHAPTER EIGHT

The Dotterel

A MORE or less typical Eurasian migrant, the dotterel winters in the Mediterranean area, North Africa, the Red Sea, Arabia and the Persian Gulf, and flies north in summer to breed somewhat locally in Northern Europe and Asia. Most of the experts, following one another rather than basing their information on actual experience, claim that the main part of the dotterel's breeding range, which extends from northern Norway through Arctic Russia and Siberia to the mouth of the River Anadyr and the Chukotskiy Mountains, is discontinuous. That is to say, they divide it into four quite distinct sections separated by gaps several hundred miles or more wide. But one wonders why the dotterel should be the only one of some sixteen Arctic-breeding waders (if one excludes the discontinuously but very far northerly breeding sanderling, knot and purple sandpiper) to have such discontinuity in its breeding range. Perhaps the explanation is that it simply has not yet been found in the areas between its known breeding localities?

Migrating dotterels visit the North Yorkshire Moors in May; the bird on the left is probably a female. This pair stayed together in the moors near Rosedale for a week or two in May 1975.

The dotterel breeds on flat mountain tops as well as on the low-lying tundra of the far north. As a result, here and there where suitable mountains provide the right habitat for it, its range reaches far south of its Arctic stronghold. Thus in the Ural Mountains its breeding range extends in a narrow band almost a thousand miles due south, as far as the high peaks of the southern Urals. Similarly, it breeds throughout a large area in the mountainous part of southern Siberia, from the mountains east of the Baikal Sea westwards to the Changaj Mountains in Mongolia and the Altai. In Scandinavia, too, it breeds on the high fells southwards into south Norway.

Interesting are the mountain-top breeding "islands" of the dotterel in various parts of Europe, some of which may even be occupied only irregularly, though here again the fact that birds are not recorded in certain years from a particular mountain range by no means proves their absence. Northern Britain forms one such breeding "island"; the eastern central Alps in Austria form another, where the birds breed very locally and rather sporadically at an altitude of 2,000 metres or slightly higher; and some of the Romanian mountains, especially the Carpathians, provide yet another dotterel breeding haunt. Until 1946 dotterels also nested on the Polish-Czechoslovak border. In 1965 breeding was proved in Switzerland, but, though birds were seen in four subsequent years, no further evidence of breeding was obtained. In 1956 dotterels were heard calling on Mount Olympus in Greece but no nest was found, and in 1959 they were seen displaying in the Wicklow Mountains, south of Dublin; again, no nest was found. In the Caucasus a pair was found breeding in 1972.

I was fortunate enough, on 19th July 1952, to my intense surprise, to discover the dotterel breeding in central Italy, in the Monte Maiella massif not far from where, unknown to me at that time, it had been recorded in 1939. Walking across the flat stony waste of the *altipiano* or high plateau of Monte Amaro, at about 2,300 metres, I was astonished to see a pair of dotterels; and even more astonished when, a few minutes later a shepherd brought me a chick, which I photographed. This was the first breeding record for anywhere in Europe south of the Alps and Carpathians. That the Maiella massif is a regular dotterel breeding locality is made likely by the fact that I found the birds there again in the following year, and in 1974 they were again proved to be breeding. They were also proved to breed there in 1975, 1976 and 1977. It remains a distinct possibility that some of the dotterel's other mountain-top haunts may be occupied regularly, but the probable breeding in Iceland in 1864 and in Alaska in 1930 is most unlikely to have been repeated.

We must conclude that the dotterel is one of those species which breeds here and there from time to time well away from its normal breeding range, and that it has permanently occupied outposts which are likewise far removed from its main stronghold. But what are we to make of the extraordinary discovery, in 1961, of two pairs of dotterel breeding at or below sea-level on recently-reclaimed polder in the older Zuider Zee in the Netherlands? This phenomenon has apparently been repeated annually since then: in 1964 at least five nests were found in East Flevoland and in 1963, on 18th May, some 130 birds were seen there. Clearly in the light of this, one must reconsider other records of dotterels breeding in low-lying areas which have hitherto been dismissed or disregarded, for example in Champagne in the eighteenth century, near Ahlsdorf in (East) Germany in 1827, in various places in Denmark in the early nineteenth century, and perhaps elsewhere.

A dotterel chick photographed in July 1952 stands among the scorched limestone fragments of the altipiano or high plateau of the Monte Maiella massif in the central Appennines, Italy—the most southerly dotterel chick ever recorded.

The dotterel leaves its extremely widespread breeding haunts for the most part towards the end of August and begins to arrive in its much more constricted winter quarters in the Middle East and North Africa in September. The peak autumn passage in Hungary is in September and October, the peak return passage in April. But it is late May or even early June before the birds arrive in their breeding haunts in the far north. The journey seems to be accomplished in groups or even sizeable flocks, and regular traditional resting places or "relay stations" are used en route where the birds may remain for days at a time, especially in autumn when they are moulting.

The distribution and migration of the dotterel in Britain has been studied in detail by Desmond Nethersole-Thompson. He concluded that the dotterel, as a "fringe" bird here on the extreme western edge of its range, has fluctuated in numbers and distribution according to changes in climate, and he suggested that, during the ten years up to the time of his writing in 1973, a worsening or cooling climate had caused it to increase in numbers and spread. Thus there is some evidence of a recent re-colonization of former breeding haunts in the Lakeland fells. New areas may even be in the process of being colonized. In 1967 the dotterel was found breeding in Sutherland and also in the south of Scotland, in Kirkcudbright. In 1969 breeding was proved in Wales.

The headquarters of the dotterel in Britain has always been the Cairngorms and the west Grampians. In this century it has bred regularly in the following Scottish counties: Perth, Angus, Aberdeen, Banff and Inverness, and probably also in Ross and Cromarty. As to total numbers, Nethersole-Thompson hazards an estimate of about seventy pairs (plus or minus ten), nesting on average annually in Britain; in years of unusually high numbers the total may have exceeded 100 pairs, while in the "thin" years of the 1930s it may have dropped below fifty pairs.

The history of the dotterel as a breeding bird in England has been studied in detail by Derek Ratcliffe (in Nethersole-Thompson 1973), who estimated that, up to about 1860, some 50 or 75 pairs may have nested, in good years, mainly on the Lakeland fells. Thereafter, until about 1900, the dotterel was a regular breeder on several Lakeland ranges, but in considerably reduced numbers. In the first quarter of the twentieth century a few pairs still attempted to breed annually, but after 1927 breeding probably ceased to occur every year, and gaps of several years between recorded nests began to appear. In the last twenty years or so a slight increase seems to have occurred, for two nests were found in 1969 and two in 1970. On average, thought Ratcliffe, a single pair might nest in England each year.

It is late April or May before dotterels arrive in England on their spring migration. In former days they were well known and common passage birds, travelling in quite large flocks or "trips" and resting in the same localities year after year. Certain Breckland heaths were favoured, hence the name "Dotterel Hall" in Cambridgeshire; some fields near the coast on the Yorkshire Wolds were visited annually, hence the "Dotterel Inn". Small trips or single birds still visit these and similar places almost annually, usually in May. There is a favourite spot on Danby Low Moor in the North Yorkshire Moors and in another locality thereabouts two birds stayed from 3rd to 11th May 1975. On autumn passage, in England, dotterels are much rarer; more often than not single birds only are recorded. On the south coast, September is the usual time for such records.

Sufficient dotterels have been ringed to show that *Ortstreue*—the instinct to return year after year to the same spot—is somewhat weak in this species. Of sixty-three adult and young Austrian dotterels ringed at their breeding place, only ten were subsequently controlled there. Of thirty-eight birds ringed by Rittinghaus in Lapland, not one was recorded as returning to its nesting fell. Dotterels ringed in Fenno-Scandinavia as young birds have been recovered on autumn passage in the Netherlands, in Algeria, in Belgium, and in Jugoslavia. In striking contrast to the principle of *Ortstreue*, a young bird ringed in Finland was recovered in May of its third year in Russia, over 4,000 kilometres to the east of its birthplace. Remarkable too is the case of the September passage dotterel ringed at Wexford, Ireland, which was recovered in the following summer on the Yenesei near Igarka, presumably still on passage, 5,600 kilometres to the east. It is difficult to suggest a figure for the breeding density of dotterels. In Scotland they may approach three pairs per square kilometre of dotterel ground in a good year; in Finnish Lapland a figure of about one per square kilometre of suitable fell has been suggested. In Arctic Russia density varies but in favoured areas figures of five or even eight to ten pairs per square kilometre have been estimated.

On the dotterel's natural predators in Britain little information has been published, but it is certainly hunted and taken on occasion by peregrine falcons and merlins, as well as foxes, while eggs and young fall prey to crows. The activities of man in the nineteenth century contributed much to the dotterel's decline in numbers and contracting breeding range in Britain. Even though some of the references to "dotterels" in accounts may refer to ringed or other plovers, it is clear that they were often killed for the table in early times. From the late eighteenth century their feathers became popular with fly fishermen. By the 1830s the collectors had moved in, and both eggs and skins were eagerly sought after, birds being shot in numbers on spring passage both in Lancashire and Yorkshire, and elsewhere. The more adventurous English collectors also pursued their predatory activities in Scandinavia: at least twenty-four clutches were collected in Lapland for John Wolley. Egg collecting continued well into the twentieth century though Nethersole-Thompson, himself an egger, argues that their activities can scarcely have caused any further decline in dotterel numbers this century. He thinks that some 300 to 350 clutches of dotterel's eggs may have been taken in Britain between 1900 and 1970.

Even so, some may think it a good thing that it is now illegal in this country to take dotterel's eggs or to disturb them while breeding. What other measures of conservation are necessary to protect this beautiful, interesting, and never very common bird? It has been maintained, though on the basis of little evidence, that old haunts are still being deserted and that increasing disturbance from hill walkers and naturalists may lead to further contractions of the bird's range. On the other hand several recent and successful Lakeland nests have been found on much frequented fells, and many of the dotterel's nesting haunts will always remain extremely remote.

The tameness of the dotterel has become almost legendary, though the pedant will point out that the sitting dotterel which one can approach and even touch is exhibiting pseudo-tameness rather than real tameness, for it has not been tamed. Occasional individual birds, of most other wader species, behave in a similar manner, but with the dotterel tight or very tight sitting is the rule. In 1909 the pioneering Swedish bird photographer Bengt Berg published an extraordinary series of photographs in a book called *My friend the dotterel*, showing a dotterel calmly incubating with one or more persons standing or sitting just by it. Another bird is portrayed taking worms from the hand and a series of photographs show a dotterel sitting on its eggs while they and the nest lining under them are raised right off the ground in the author's hand and held in his lap!

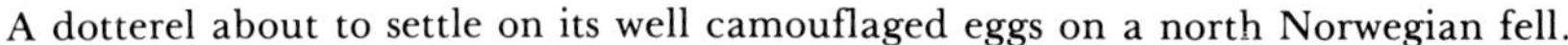

A dotterel about to settle on its well camouflaged eggs on a north Norwegian fell.

The most commonly heard note of the dotterel is given in flight; it is a rapidly repeated "peep peep peep" which carries far though it is not in fact very loud. Other notes described by Nethersole-Thompson are a sharp explosive "ting", and a "skirr" which Rittinghaus described as "dru". The female's song, uttered in flight, is a rapidly repeated "pit pit pit". Other notes are used at the nest, by the male when looking after young, and during distraction display. This frequently occurs when a bird is disturbed at the nest. It flutters as if helpless along the ground, falling onto its breast, or onto one side, flapping its wings and often spreading its tail or dragging it along the ground.

Not only is the dotterel sometimes polyandrous, one female mating with more than one male, but the role of the sexes are more often than not reversed during most of the breeding cycle. It is the rather dull-coloured male which normally incubates the eggs and tends the young single-handed, at least in some cases leaving the female free to solicit and stimulate other males. It was the Nethersole-Thompsons who first proved the dotterel's polyandry—in 1934. On the 10th June in that year they found a clutch of three unusually marked eggs which they realized at once had been laid by a female, which they had named "Blackie", who had laid a similarly unique clutch in the same place the year before. These eggs were slightly set and incubation must have started on about 3rd or 4th June. On 25th June they found another clutch of uniquely marked eggs— Blackie's again, indubitably—which had been incubated about ten or twelve days. Thus Blackie had mated with a first cock and laid a clutch of eggs for him to incubate; then, about eleven days later, she had laid a second clutch after mating with a second cock.

Dotterels begin to arrive on the tops in early May but the date of pairing and egg-laying varies considerably from year to year, depending on the amount of snow cover and the weather conditions. They probably begin to breed when they are two years old, that is, in their third calendar year. Pairs are formed from displaying groups of from three to six birds. Thereafter, scrapes are made independently by both cock and hen, but it is the hen which at this stage carries out the "advertisement" or song flight, by flying high over the hill tops with alternating glides and rapidly repeated wing beats, calling "pit pit pit" or "wit wit wit". The territory is now formed and will be vigorously defended, especially by the incubating cock, against other dotterels.

The nest making and nest making ceremonies of the dotterel are similar to those of other plovers. The first scraping movements of male and female are uncoordinated and make no impression on the ground. But soon a hollow is scraped out with the feet, and the breast rotated in it, by each bird separately and by both together. In the intervals between spells of scraping the hen or the cock picks up pieces of grass or moss and throws them over its shoulder. This ritualized material tossing, as in other plovers, provides materials for lining the nest. In the case of the dotterel, it is often followed by copulation.

A migrant dotterel in Yorkshire in May.

The nest itself, that is the scrape in which the hen chooses to lay her eggs, is normally out in the open with an all-round view, and usually on a bare flat ridge or mountain top. It may be in a patch of moss, deer sedge or mat grass, or simply among stones. The nest hollow is usually sparsely lined with moss, lichen, blaeberry or crowberry leaves or grass. An elaborate egg-laying ceremony, similar to the scrape making ceremony, often accompanies the laying of a dotterel pair's first egg. The eggs, which are not laid at any particular time of day, are produced at intervals of from twenty-four to thirty hours. In the Cairngorms Nethersole-Thompson found that egg-laying might begin as early as 9th May in a warm spring or as late as 13th June in a cold one. The mean date of laying the first egg was 27th May. The dotterel's egg is ovate in shape, not pointed as in waders laying clutches of four, and the usual clutch is three. The eggs are olive brown or buff-brown in ground colour, thickly spotted with black or brownish-black blotches, streaks and spots. The incubation period is about twenty-six days, and the young fly some twenty-six days after hatching, having been cared for or accompanied by the male bird alone. The females form "hen-parties" while the males are still incubating, and apparently leave the breeding areas before the males.

Hatching success in the dotterel appears to be high; 56 chicks hatched from 61 Scottish eggs (90.8 per cent) but only 33 of them (59.8 per cent) lived beyond the end of the first week. In some countries, or at certain times, egg-losses through deep and lasting snow cover can be very heavy. Thus one dotterel pair in Austria raised only one young from two clutches each of three eggs, and in 1969 no chicks at all were produced from five clutches of eggs.

CHAPTER NINE

The Golden Plover

COMMON as a breeding bird on much of the moorland and mountain of northern and western Britain, the golden plover also winters in large numbers in lowland Britain. Abroad, its range is distinctly limited, for it is restricted as a breeding bird in western Europe to Iceland, the Faroes, Britain and Ireland, Bear Island (?), Norway, Sweden, and parts of Finland, while it occurs locally in small numbers in Denmark and West Germany. Further east, in the Soviet Union, it breeds in Latvia and Estonia, doubtfully in the region of Leningrad and Novgorod, but certainly in the Kola, Kanin and Yamal Peninsulas and eastwards as far as the River Yenesei.

On the evidence of ringing recoveries, British breeding golden plovers seldom move far in winter from their summer haunts. Up till 1958, 16 out of 537 golden plovers ringed as chicks in Britain had been recovered. None of them were outside Britain and none were more than 100 miles from where they had been ringed as chicks. Since then a chick ringed in June in Sutherland has been recovered in February in Portugal. Other populations habitually migrate over substantial distances. Icelandic breeding golden plovers winter in the British Isles, especially Ireland, but also in western France, the Iberian Peninsula and Morocco. Norwegian birds ringed as chicks have been recovered in Holland; and adults on autumn passage in Norway have been recovered in Portugal and Morocco. Finnish bred birds have been recovered in France and Morocco, and chicks ringed in Russia have been recovered as adults in France and Italy.

Recoveries in Britain of golden plovers ringed elsewhere show that our birds are reinforced in winter by substantial contingents from Iceland. In the period 1906-63 a total of 77 foreign-ringed golden plovers were recovered in Britain; 61 of them had been ringed in Iceland, a single bird had been ringed in the Faroes, the other 15 had been ringed on passage in the Netherlands and were probably hatched in Scandinavia or Russia (Hudson 1965).

In Holland intensive ringing of passage and wintering golden plovers has yielded a great deal of information. Between 1911 and 1970 a grand total of 13,319 golden plovers were ringed in the Netherlands, 680 of which had been recovered by 1972. The numbers recovered in each country were as follows (Speek 1973):

Netherlands	168	Germany	3
British Isles	21	Poland	3
Belgium	11	Denmark	66
France	177	Norway	9
Iberian Peninsula	113	Sweden	12
Italy	17	Finland	2
North Africa	33	European Soviet Union	40
Iceland	1	Asiatic Soviet Union	4

Every ringing programme, besides ringing hitherto unringed birds, also provides recoveries of birds ringed elsewhere, though these birds, released after checking the ring number and perhaps re-ringing, are properly speaking referred to as "controlled" rather than "recovered". The numbers of golden plovers ringed abroad in different countries and recovered or controlled in the Netherlands, up to 31st December 1973, were as follows (Glutz von Blotzheim 1975):

Ireland	1	Germany	2
Britain	21	Poland	1
Belgium	13	Denmark	69
France	189	Norway	11
Iberian Peninsula	122	Sweden	8
Italy	19	Finland	2
North Africa	31	Soviet Union	45
Iceland	1		

All the golden plovers ringed in Holland and all the ringed golden plovers recovered or controlled in Holland are either adults or full grown juveniles. No golden plovers have bred in that country since 1937, but the bird is a common passage migrant and winter visitor, and modern ringers, as so often, have been able to adopt the techniques of the old-time trappers. For centuries the golden plover, well known in Frisia as the *wilster*, has been trapped there along the Waddensee shore in the north of the province. Netting was undertaken in open grassy pastures using a large clap-net up to 24 metres long by 2½-3 metres wide, to catch the birds in flight. The trapper stood behind a screen of some kind some 30 metres from the net. To attract the birds he used a whistle to imitate golden plover calls and usually employed a live lapwing or two and a golden plover tied to sticks so that he could make them flap their wings and appear to alight by pulling a string. Up to twenty or so stuffed golden plovers were set out on the grass to act as decoys. As a flock came sweeping in to settle the net was pulled up and over them. Twenty at once was quite often achieved; in the winter of 1938-39 it was calculated that 16,185 birds were caught by 67 catchers. In that season the ringers went out catching wilsters and 296 birds were ringed. So began the scientific trapping of wilsters. Instead of being killed and sent to market, mostly in England, they were ringed and released (Haverschmidt 1943; Eenhuistra 1973).

Male lapwings in territorial confrontation

Migrating grey plovers in summer plumage in August

The golden plover seems to be an unsuccessful species, suffering a steadily shrinking range and a concomitant decline in numbers. Certainly this is true of the western and southern parts of the range. K. H. Voous (1960) tells us that "the western European breeding area (Britain, Netherland, northern Germany), which formerly was much more extensive and continuous than it now is, has the character of a glacial relic. Moreover, the species as a whole is given the character of a relic species by a distribution which for an Arctic bird is very limited . . .".

The numerical decline of the golden plover, which has been linked with climatic changes and in many areas to land reclamation for agriculture and to forestry schemes, both of which have brought about the large scale destruction of its heathland or peat bog habitat, has been recorded in all parts of the range habitually assigned to its so-called "southern" sub-species, *Pluvialis apricaria apricaria*. Thus in Ireland it was said in (Ruttledge) 1966 to be breeding "sparsely" on mountains in 5 or 6 counties in the north and north-west, in two of which it also bred locally on low-lying moors barely above sea level; and there were a few pairs in another county in low-lying terrain. Yet around 1900 it was reported as breeding in 17 counties. In Britain, Ratcliffe (1976) has provided detailed evidence for decrease in many areas while conceding that in others numbers have been maintained. Although documentation is poor, the conclusion seems to be that the golden plover is declining in many areas, including Wales and parts of the Pennines, though since 1950 a colony of perhaps 10 or 12 pairs has become established on Dartmoor, where the species had been virtually extinct for more than a hundred years. In Denmark the golden plover was once a widespread breeding species, but there were only 47-78 pairs left in North and West Jutland in 1937-39 and a mere 13-17 pairs in 1972. In Belgium a few pairs bred in the Hautes Fagnes between Eupen and Malmédy until 1910, and in several localities in Holland golden plovers were still breeding until the 1920s. The last nest in the Netherlands was found in Friesland in 1937. In Poland and East Germany the species has not bred since the nineteenth century, when it was widespread, apart from a single attempt in Poland.

Our almost total lack of knowledge of the actual numbers of breeding golden plovers is illustrated by the disagreement among recent estimates. In 1973 Parslow put the total British and Irish population at between 1,001 and 10,000 breeding pairs, but in the very same year Prater was credited (Glutz von Blotzheim 1975) with an estimate of from 28,400 to 38,650 pairs. The same author, in conjunction with D. A. Ratcliffe, estimated on the basis of *Atlas* data (Sharrock 1976) that there were 30,000 pairs but this number may well have been over-optimistic.

In 1974 the results of two detailed studies of breeding golden plover numbers were published; they are the only ones so far undertaken, to my knowledge. One related to the Peak District of Britain, forming the southern end of the Pennines, the other to the southern Norwegian coastal population of golden plovers in the area called Jaeren, south of Stavanger in the county of Rogaland. In the Peak District, Yalden could find no evidence of any substantial decline in the total breeding population, estimated at 380-400 pairs by counting birds apparently holding territories. With the help of members of the Rogaland section of the Norwegian Ornithological Society, Byrkjedal managed, after preliminary counts in 1968-71, to carry out a complete census of the golden plovers in Jaeren in 1974. He found that counting was only really reliable when the golden plovers had unfledged young, that is, since eggs hatch in that area around 31st May, in June. The total number of pairs in his study area was 213, and no evidence was found of a decline, though there was general agreement that this now rather isolated Norwegian population represents the remains of a much larger nineteenth-century population which was then spread over a wider area.

Bathing golden plover.

Surprisingly, perhaps, British ornithologists have preferred the difficult business of winter censusing, instead of any attempt to census breeding pairs of golden plovers on a national scale. Apparently the original idea was to devote the autumn of 1976-7 to identifying the normal wintering localities, and to follow this up with a nationwide census of wintering flocks on a chosen weekend in January 1977 (Youngman and Fuller 1976; Lloyd 1977 and 1978).

The planned census was incomplete, but it was estimated that in January 1977 there were about 195,000 golden plovers in Britain and Northern Ireland, nearly 153,000 of them in England. During the following winter, that of 1977-8, several nationwide counts of golden plovers were made—in November, late December and February. Between 147,000 and 190,000 birds were recorded, and the organiser of the survey concluded that the total winter population could number 200,000 birds, a total which was the same as the Irish Wildbird Conservancy's estimate of the number of golden plovers wintering in Eire, thus making a grand total of 400,000 birds for Britain and Ireland. Even if all the British breeding birds were among these flocks, their size implies that many of our wintering birds are immigrants from outside Britain, no doubt from Iceland, Scandinavia and Russia.

Photographing golden plovers in winter is no easy task, though the fact that they repair year after year to the same area and even to the same fields does make things easier. Several mornings in succession at the end of November 1971 I ensconced myself in a hide I had left for several days at the edge of a grassy field near the north shore of the Humber where golden plovers habitually wintered. The first morning, which was cold and frosty, I spent from soon after sunrise at 0800 hours until midday half-frozen in the hide. At first there was nothing save a distant sparrow cheep from the farm, then the note of a passing skylark. But, ten minutes after entering the hide, I heard the melodious but subdued whistling call-note of a golden plover, twice repeated in the distance: "too-*ee*, too-*ee*". More calls came later, including the "wee-erty-weer" note commonly heard in the breeding season. Birds flew distantly in groups, then began to settle, but always far out of photographic range. In flight they nearly always called, using a sustained high-pitched "peee" or "cheee" as well as the more usual "too-*ee*". The next morning I soon had some twenty golden plovers feeding scattered over the grass, but far from the hide. Common gulls were repeatedly chasing them for worms. I watched a golden plover pulling out a large worm, running backwards a few paces to do so, then swallowing it. A bird some 45 yards away looks at me suspiciously, then flies off, hide shy at that distance! Then a passing crow makes the entire flock fly and I notice that there are now over 50 of them. No exposures made that morning either! Two days later I obtained some photographs of a feeding bird at 30 yards range with the big telephoto lens. Four further mornings in the same hide yielded equally unsatisfactory results—a few distant pictures with the long lens, scarcely worth printing. It was only years later, after many more hours in hides, that I was fortunate in choosing a superb sunny day in January, erecting my hide slap in the middle of the field, and obtaining a nice series of close-up portraits of feeding golden plovers. My success on that occasion seems to have been due to the fact that there were cows in the field, all round the hide, and the golden plovers were feeding among them.

A winter flock of golden plovers in a grass pasture near the Humber. Once they begin to feed, the flock will disperse over the field.

Those winter days with the golden plovers taught me a great deal about them. I found that virtually all the calls used in the breeding season are also used in winter. Even the beautiful haunting cadence of the song flight call "er-*pee*-er" was occasionally forthcoming. I found, too, that the golden plovers kept themselves in a fairly tight flock when flying about and when resting—which they nearly always did on plough, where they were more or less invisible—but scattered right over the area when feeding, so that each bird was then apparently no longer so much part of a flock, as an individual on its own. They seemed to feed almost exclusively on earthworms, and were constantly chased by common and black-headed gulls and sometimes by lapwings, all of which tried to steal their worms from them.

Were these wintering goldies—as we habitually call them—the same birds as those I have watched and photographed year after year in the North Yorkshire Moors, 50 miles away to the north? Only colour ringing could answer this question, and this would entail a major disturbance of the birds, either by trapping adults or searching for and catching the chicks. Instead I have been content to watch them, either from a hide or from the car, which one can park by a moorland track in such a way as to be able to watch 3 or 4 pairs at once. Not that goldie watching is always full of interest and excitement. Far from it. On 15th April 1978 I kept a pair under observation for 3½ hours continuously. They were on their breeding territory and their behaviour was, in my experience, quite typical. Keeping always a few yards apart, never nearer each other than several feet, one bird running a few paces then the other, they never did anything else save feed, except once when the female called "chew-ee" several times, and on two occasions when she performed a crouching run away from the male with head held down and rump raised, as if to invite coition. But the male ignored her. Otherwise there was no sign at all that the birds were a breeding pair, no visits to scrapes, no interaction between the two birds, no song from the male. That was watching in luxury, from the car. My longest spell in a hide on a goldie's territory was ten hours; on that occasion not a single photograph was obtained!

On the moors, though an occasional bird or birds may be found in winter, the goldie-watching season really starts in February, when pairs of birds may from time to time be seen on their territories, especially in the early morning, though some birds are not yet paired. Thus in 1975 on 16th February, when the ground was frozen hard and a vicious wind blew under a cold grey sky, and the only passerine bird about was a solitary snow bunting, a short walk over some of the traditional goldie territories revealed two pairs already in possession. But there was also a party of three birds which settled for a time, then flew off. Later that morning two other groups of three birds were seen. It looked as if the males were not yet in full summer plumage. A week later, in freezing fog, two birds were seen briefly flying over one of the territories but not settling, and a party of 6 birds were feeding on the traditional extra-territorial feeding ground half a mile away. By 8th March that year the full song flight was heard and one pair at least spent most of the day in their territory, but no activity was seen other than feeding. In 1976, on 20th March, after a very hard frost which would have made scrape making quite impossible every territory was occupied, most of the birds just standing facing the cold wind, hunched and inactive.

By early April the North Yorkshire Moors goldies spend most of the time on their territories, and they apparently remain there at night too, though they also frequent the above mentioned "neutral" feeding ground nearby from time to time. Thus on 7th April 1976 in the evening no birds were found on their territories, but 10-15 were feeding on the neutral ground in a loose flock. Territories are defended in the first place by the male bird, which, if an intruding goldie lands in its territory, will fly at it and chase it off, accompanied by its mate. All three birds may fly round together for a time. In some years territories have been held by single birds, apparently males hoping for a mate. I have found no evidence of a phenomenon reported from northeast Scotland, where apparently suitable breeding terrain is in short supply, of different pairs successively occupying the same territory in the same season (Parr 1979).

It is an open question how far the beautiful song flight of the male goldie has a territorial function, as for example claimed by Rittinghaus (1969), and how far it is part of the so-called "courtship" ceremonies. It is usually ignored when heard from overhead by a bird on its territory. It is normally an individual affair, but one bird seems to stimulate another, so that two or three are often heard at once. It is perhaps more frequent early in the day, but may be heard at any time, and it seems to come in spurts followed by lulls. Sometimes two or three birds fly together while singing; on 15th April 1978 six birds flew over me together, at least four, and I think all of them, were performing the song flight.

A golden plover performs its territorial song flight over the North Yorkshire Moors. It flies up with rapidly beating wings, then suddenly begins to glide, maintaining itself in the air with a slow wing beat and long intervals between beats (a frequency of about one beat per second instead of the normal ten or more) while repeatedly uttering a loud sweet whistling call "ter *wee*-er, ter *wee*-er", the second part long drawn out, haunting, almost melancholic, nostalgic. After doing this during two or three aerial circuits around the territory some 100 feet above ground, usually with a break or two while it briefly resumes normal flight, the bird suddenly plummets nearly vertically downwards calling as it lands, with wings still upstretched, "wy-erty wer", or "wy-erty wer erty wer". Sometimes two or three birds perform this song flight in company—then the moors resound to the most beautiful chorus imaginable of soft melodious whistles. The favoured time for this song flight is early morning. It is one of the wildest, loveliest, loneliest of all bird songs.

No wonder in some places the goldie has been called the invisible piper (German *Pfeifer*) or whistler over the moors. On the Swedish island of Öland, where a much studied sea level goldie population nests on the flat stony heath called the Alvar, it is known as the *Alvar-grimen* or ghost of the heath (Steiniger 1959). Especially when more than one bird is singing the air becomes full of their melodic whistling cadences, yet the birds themselves, perhaps because they are flying slowly, with few wing beats, are extremely hard to see, even with binoculars. The complete cycle of a goldie's song flight seems to be as follows. First the bird flies up from the ground in normal flight with rapid wing beats calling loudly "kee-kee-kee" or "chee-chee-chee", the note which is also uttered in flight when a male chases another bird out of its territory. It gains height, then changes to a gliding flight with slow wing-beats, often drifting sideways with the wind. The rate is approximately one wing beat per second. The legs are often allowed to dangle. Each time the bird flaps its wings it emits a loud whistling call "per-*pee*-oo"; some birds add a syllable, "per-*pee*-oo-loo,,. This call carries far and lasts for up to two or three seconds. While doing this the bird flies round its territory and beyond it, passing over the territories of many of its neighbours, though without eliciting any response from them. Every now and then the slow wing beats are abandoned and the bird reverts to normal flight, using rapid wing beats to gain height. The song ceases momentarily while this is done, then recommences. After a minute or so, or sometimes two or three or perhaps several minutes, the bird stops singing, calls loudly "kee-er, kee-er, kee-er", and dramatically plummets down to earth, landing in its territory. Immediately on landing, it stretches its wings up over its back and calls "wy-erty-wer, wy-erty-wer".

Trying to photograph goldies performing their song flight is no simple matter. On 6th May 1973 I awoke in my Volkswagen caravette at 0545 to the sound of goldie song; a very low sun shone above the distant haze-enshrouded sea somewhere near Whitby. Getting out of the car, I was greeted with the loud "chee, chee" alarm note of a goldie invisible on the ground. The first lark goes up, a meadow pipit utters its high-pitched silvery "zilp, zilp, zilp", and a deeply guttural grouse shouts from afar. A cool south-west breeze blows into my face with a tang to it like sea-spray; wisps of low fast-moving cloud scud across the sun. It dims. I notice that the sky is dark over the western hills towards Rosedale and Farndale. This is suggestive, then suddenly sinister; for banks of low cold mist are rolling in over the moors. The sun is at issue with cloud and fog; its radiant warmth only intermittently pierces the dank mountain air. It becomes dark and cold for a moment, then brilliantly sunny and warm; sometimes parts of my moorland surroundings are bright, parts dull. I pace the track trying to keep warm. Since I left the car with the long lens mounted on a heavy tripod no goldie has sung! The wind is cold now but scented as it moans gently around my tripod. Only after half an hour do the mist banks thin out and the sun shines in a partly blue sky. The landscape is soft, hazy, watery, with beautiful colour variations. A goldie is up high above me at last and I manage to keep it in the viewfinder long enough to take a series of photos as it flies overhead lit by the early morning sun. I see the bird's beak open in the viewfinder before the sound of the first syllable of the song comes to me. But, while my fingers rapidly freeze, a great cloud bank swirls around me from the west. Towards the shooting bothy a brilliant sun is still climbing up the sky; the distant ridges recede into the haze. The dark, strongly back-lit foreground of heather and silvery grass and rush-clumps contrasts with the glassy puddles on the moorland road. But the splendid scene is menaced by the racing white mist clouds which are soon almost overhead, backed by a threatening dark grey cloud bank which spreads towards me. Soon the predominant colours of the moorland in spring, always restrained—dark sepia heather, grey-white burnt heather patches, and buff coloured rush tufts—are altogether obliterated. One more brief song flight and the sky is overcast. At 0730 I am breakfasting in the car, surrounded by a uniform, monotonous grey cloud. No further photography was possible that day.

Between late March and late April the goldies, if you are very lucky and persistent, may be seen making their nest scrapes and mating. The male initiates these activities, and an unpaired male in a territory has been seen to make several scrapes and scrape in them repeatedly, without any encouragement or aid from a female. In 1975 a pair called "the crater pair" from a wartime bomb crater in their territory had 6 scrapes within a circle 60 yards across; but in the event the female chose to lay in the previous year's nest, which had been left untouched and unscraped in. The male visits his scrapes only very occasionally, probably as little as once or twice only in a day. He may visit one briefly, or he may "do the rounds", scraping for a time in each scrape. At the scrape he utters a characteristic soft "pip, pip, pip", fluffing out his throat feathers with each "pip". A male I watched on 3rd April 1974 visited four scrapes in succession. Sometimes he stopped and went briefly through the scraping movements in a mere hollow in the ground. At one of the scrapes he picked up twigs, pieces of grass, or moss in his bill and threw them over his shoulder for some minutes; at another he did no pecking at all. Once at a scrape, either bird may stay for several minutes; even for 10 or 15 minutes. The bird's time at the scrape is usually unequally divided between sitting in the scrape wriggling violently or scraping with its feet, the wings being half extended and tail held up, or standing at the scrape picking up dry grass and other fragments and throwing them back. This pecking and throwing may be indulged in by both birds together for 5 minutes or more at a stretch. The goldie pair is by no means so demonstrative at the nest scrape as either the lapwing or the ringed plover; there is little real displaying, though I have seen a male adopt a crouching gait as he makes way for his mate at the scrape.

April 1975. The male golden plover had momentarily settled onto the egg the female bird had laid in the nest scrape earlier that same morning—the first egg of the clutch. When she approaches, he leaves the scrape in a "hunched" attitude and she takes a turn on the egg.

Coition in the golden plover is accomplished with the minimum of fuss and is in my experience very rarely seen. It is all over in 6-10 seconds. The male moves up to the female with the usual short runs plus pauses; the last run up to her is faster and his tail is somewhat depressed. He stands on the female's back for three to five seconds, then several times vigorously depresses his tail; then runs off forwards.

On the North Yorkshire Moors the first golden plover's eggs do not seem to be laid before mid-April. In 1975 three neighbouring birds laid their first egg on 19th-20th April and a fourth had one egg on 23rd April. In 1974 a nest with 2 eggs on 21st April points to a first egg laid on about 19th April. The earliest chicks I have ever seen there were very recently hatched on 14th May 1972, which means that the clutch of eggs was probably completed on about 18th April and the first egg laid on 10-12th April. The nests are not always easy to find. If the sitting bird is alone in the territory it will fly low directly off the eggs when one is any distance from about 20 to well over 100 yards away. Very occasionally a sitting bird will sit much tighter; on one occasion only I found a bird which was so "tame" that you could almost touch her while she incubated. If the sitting bird's mate is present with it in the territory it will normally call the sitting bird off the nest when the intruder first appears in sight. In these circumstances the nest is almost impossible to find. The sitting bird slips quietly off unseen, walks some distance away, then begins to repeat the alarm note "plee, plee", joining its mate in standing about calling until both fly off together.

Injury feigning is rarely seen on the North Yorkshire Moors, even when birds have young. Indeed the only time I have recorded it was on 23rd April 1975 when a bird flew up from a nest containing one egg when I was only a few paces away, dangling a leg and wing fluttering as if it had a broken or damaged wing. In north Norway I have seen a bird put off four eggs flying away like this, so that at first I scarcely recognized it as a golden plover, but imagined it to be some kind of crake. In the case of both the ringed plover and the golden plover injury feigning is far more common and more elaboate among northern populations than in Britain. Another golden plover in north Norway, also with four eggs, gave a sustained and truly remarkable display of injury feigning every time I visited her nest. She actually kept it up for nearly half an hour while I moved the hide and photographed her. When I was at the nest she would approach me with a creeping run, then flap and flutter away from me with lowered head and depressed tail, which was also fanned out. One or both wings would be outstretched and held out for some time. All these movements were slow and deliberate, the bird not more than 10 yards away from me the whole time. Williamson (1948) described three different lure displays employed by Faroese golden plovers with eggs or small chicks.

Injury feigning by golden plover, Norway.

Nest and eggs of golden plover.

Goldies are sometimes remarkably easy, but more often rather difficult, to photograph at the nest. The hide must be moved up very slowly, especially in the final stages when it is moved closer than 10 yards to the nest. In 1975 I found a female which was totally unconcerned by the hide and camera, and watched her incubating at close quarters for 7 hours. She sat very still, though her pulse caused her whole body to vibrate. It varied from a rate of about 120 to a mere 70 beats per minute. She dozed off, but every time her eyes closed she opened them with a head-shake, as if on guard duty and not allowed to sleep. Every now and then — once or twice in an hour — she got up and changed position, moving approximately 45° each time, sometimes clockwise, sometimes anti-clockwise. This movement was in fact a very complex piece of behaviour, often preceded and followed by pecking at twigs and grass stems near the nest. The bird gets up, moves round, rhythmically moves its whole body to and fro, with the breast held downwards, then makes scraping movements with its legs, holding the tail up, then shuffles vigorously sideways to and fro as it lowers itself onto the eggs in the new position.

The golden plover's four eggs usually hatch more or less simultaneously, though gaps of up to two days between the first and last egg have been recorded. The adults remove the egg-shells and, as usual with waders, the young have to fend for themselves from the start by finding their own food. Both parents tend the young and may divide the brood between them. The chicks fly about four or five weeks after hatching but there is virtually no information available about hatching success. The longest living golden plover so far recorded was ringed as an adult in Holland on 14th January 1952 and recovered in Britain on 15th December 1962.

CHAPTER TEN

The Grey Plover

THE DUTCH and the French rather charmingly call this bird the "silver plover"; in North America, more prosaically, it is the "black-bellied plover". Its Arctic breeding grounds are more remote from Britain than those of any other European wader because, for some unexplained reason, it breeds neither in Greenland nor Spitsbergen, where apparently suitable habitats certainly exist, and where other birds of the far north, for example knots and sanderling, breed in large numbers. In North America the grey plover's breeding range extends from the northern coast of Alaska right along the coasts and islands of the Northwest Territories in Canada, as far north as Banks Island and the northwestern tip of Baffin Island, as far east as the southwestern shore of Baffin Island, and as far south as Southampton Island on the north side of Hudson Bay.

In the Old World the breeding range approaches considerably nearer Britain, but even so, the nearest localities are the Kanin Penisula and Kolguev Island, some two thousand miles away from southern England. Thence the grey plover breeds on a narrow strip of coastal tundra right along the north coast of Siberia eastwards to the Bering Sea, never penetrating southwards off the genuine tundra nor nesting on any of the islands in the Arctic Ocean except for those, like Kolguev, Vaigach and Wrangel Islands, which are relatively close to the mainland.

From this constricted, at most five-hundred-mile wide breeding range, the grey plover migrates southwards in the autumn to the shores of every continent and indeed of almost the entire world. It is one of the greatest migrants. In winter, grey plovers are found in the Caribbean, on both coasts of Central and South America as far as Chile and Argentina, the Pacific Islands, the coasts of western Europe including Britain, right round the shores of Africa, India, southern Japan, China and much of the northern half of Australia. The most southerly example so far recorded was apparently a bird on Macquarie Island, five hundred miles south of New Zealand, on 24th February 1964. However, the grey plover is by no means spread out thinly and evenly over this enormous area, even though it is perhaps more often met with in ones and twos in winter than in large flocks. In Europe and Africa there is a definite concentration of wintering grey plovers, and there are also gaps where few are to be found. Thus 5-8,000 have been counted in January-February in the British Isles, mainly on the south and east coasts; some 6,000 are thought to winter on the Channel and Atlantic coasts of France; up to 2,000 in the Iberian Peninsula; some 2,500 in the Netherlands; and 20-40,000 on the Atlantic coasts of Morocco and Mauretania. On the other hand a mere hundred individuals winter on the North Sea coasts of Germany, and perhaps not many more than two or three thousand in the entire Mediterranean Sea, mostly in Tunisia.

Within the British Isles, the wintering population of grey plovers is not at all evenly spread. In the years after 1968 the British Trust for Ornithology and the Royal Society for the Protection of Birds organized an enquiry into the birds of British estuaries which showed that there were two main wintering areas for the grey plover, each with over 1,000 birds: the Swale estuary in Kent and the Wash. Over half the wintering population was found on the east coast between Lincolnshire and Kent. The peak count of grey plovers in each of the three full years of this survey was in January-February; the total numbers counted were as follows (Prater 1971, 1972, 1973, 1974):

January 1971	5,569
February 1972	7,350
February 1973	8,281

Whether or not these figures represent a real increase in grey plover numbers must remain in considerable doubt; an increase in the enthusiasm, efficiency and perhaps numbers of the counters may be the true explanation. Nor can they be regarded as more than minima, for many birds must certainly have gone uncounted.

Grey plover at Gibraltar Point, Lincolnshire, 2nd October, 1975.

The autumn migration of the grey plover in Europe takes a markedly western direction and the birds show a distinct liking for coasts. Presumably the flocks which build up in British estuaries and on the Atlantic coast of France in August are made up of birds from the breeding grounds along the Russian Arctic coast from the Kanin to the Taimyr Peninsulas. Highly suggestive in this respect is the record of an adult bird caught and ringed in the Vendée in western France on 19th September 1967 which was recovered in the Taimyr Peninsula on 8th June 1969. Many of these Russian breeding birds must begin their autumn migration by flying west-south-west along the coast; then southwest as far as Britain and France; finally turning south-south-west to reach the West African coast. This autumn migration is initiated by the old birds, which begin to leave the tundra in mid-July, followed by young birds, which travel much more slowly, from mid-August. Thus in Denmark two peaks in grey plover numbers occur in autumn; the first, of adults, in August; the second, of young birds, in October. The adults migrate without delay, many of them still retaining their summer plumage—I recall the striking black bellies of most of the birds in a 100-strong flock I photographed at the Pointe d'Arcay on the west coast of France on 24th August. By that date some birds will have reached the Banc d'Arguin on the Mauretanian coast; by mid-September birds have been reported from South Africa.

While the coast is certainly preferred by the grey plover as a migration route, there is an overland migration as well and, curiously enough, this occurs rather late in the autumn and is undertaken in the main by young birds. At Cambridge Sewage Farm between 1926 and 1955 the peak date for the autumn passage of grey plovers was 5th October (Nisbet 1957), and Heinrich Dathe of Leipzig found that, in his part of Saxony, maximum numbers occurred in the first half of October; he thought that they were almost all young birds.

In much of western Europe, at any rate, the return migration of the grey plover in spring extends over a considerably shorter period than the autumn migration. Thus in Saxony Dathe (1949) recorded birds in spring between 16th April and 31st May, a total of 46 days; whereas the autumn migration in Saxony lasted from 21st August to 26th November, 98 days. Moreover, on autumn migration the grey plover is usually much more numerous than in spring. In Holland and England the spring passage of grey plovers peaks at round 18th-20th May, whereas at Archangel the average date over nineteen years was 22nd May. Birds arrive on their breeding grounds in the tundra between the end of May and mid-June.

Recoveries of ringed birds bear out this general picture of grey plover migration. Virtually all recoveries save one fit in with the general pattern of a southwesterly mainly coastal migration in autumn and a spring return along the same route (Branson and Minton 1976). The single exception is the remarkable case of a bird ringed in Romania on 18th October 1969 which was recovered in South Africa on 23rd August 1970 (Glutz von Blotzheim 1975). It may have followed a more easterly "inland" route, but so far there have been no Mediterranean recoveries of grey plovers except at the extreme western end of that sea.

Although the very first discovery of a grey plover's nest was made on 26th June 1843 in the Taimyr Peninsula by the German explorer Middendorf, it was British ornithologists or travellers who made the main contribution to our knowledge of its breeding biology in the nineteenth and early twentieth centuries, even though this took the form of shooting every adult bird to which they could approach near enough, and taking all the clutches of eggs they could lay their hands on. Earliest of these bird hunters and collectors were Messrs. H. Seebohm (1901) and J. A. Harvie-Brown (1905), who set out in March 1875 to investigate and collect specimens of the bird life of the lower reaches of the River Petchora at a time when no British egg collector had set eyes on the eggs of the grey plover, little stint, sanderling, curlew sandpiper or knot. They succeeded in bringing little stint's and grey plover's eggs back to England in the fond belief that they were the first to discover these two species breeding; an expedition a good deal further east in Arctic Russia to the River Yenesei or the Taimyr Peninsula would have been necessary before they could have met with breeding sanderlings, knots or curlew sandpipers.

Preening and wing stretching are a most important activity for every bird. This grey plover has partly stretched its right wing and the light has caused its rather indistinct white wing bar. It had been preening and resumed this immediately after wing stretching. Note that the leg is extended at the same time as the wing, evidently involuntarily.

It was on 22nd June on the tundras on the east bank of the Petchora that Seebohm and Harvie-Brown with their Samoyed hunters made their first murderous onslaught on the grey plover (Seebohm 1901):

> ". . . the Samoyede tramped the ground systematically, and after more than an hour's search found a nest on one of the dry tussocky ridges intersecting the bog, containing four eggs about the size and shape of those of the golden plover, but more like those of the lapwing in colour. The nest was a hollow, evidently scratched, perfectly round, somewhat deep, and containing a handful of broken slender twigs and reindeer-moss. Harvie-Brown concealed himself as well as he could behind a ridge, to lie in wait for the bird returning to the nest, and after half an hour's watching shot a veritable grey plover. Soon afterwards another of our men found a second nest, also containing four eggs, in an exactly similar situation. Harvie-Brown took this nest also in hand, and in about an hour succeeded in shooting the female. The third nest was found by the Samoyede. This time I lay down behind a ridge some thirty yards from the nest, and after waiting a quarter of an hour caught sight of the bird on the top of a distant tussock. Presently she ran nearer to another ridge, looked round, and then ran on to the next, until she finally came within fifty yards of where I was lying. I had just made up my mind to risk a shot when she must have caught sight of me, and flew right away. In a quarter of an hour I caught sight of her again, approaching by short stages as before, but from an opposite direction. I must have been in full sight of her. When she approached within fifty yards of me, as near as I could guess, I fired at her with No. 4 shot and missed. I remained reclining where I was, with little hope that she would try a third time to approach the nest, and whiled away the time with watching a Buffon's Skua through my glass as it cautiously approached in my direction. Turning my head round suddenly I caught sight of the grey plover running towards the nest within fifty yards of me. I lifted my gun and fired again, but was so nervous that I missed her a second time. I was so vexed that I got up and walked towards the skua, which still remained *in statu quo*. I missed a shot at it too, spent some time in a vain search for its nest, and returned to my old quarters. In ten minutes I saw the grey plover flying up. It took a wheel in my direction, coming almost within shot, and evidently took stock of me, and satisfied itself that I was a harmless animal practising with blank cartridge, and having no evil design upon its eggs. It alighted about fifty yards beyond the nest, and approached less timidly than before. When it came within fifty yards of me I fired, this time with No. 6 shot, and laid the poor bird upon its back. As we returned to our boat Harvie-Brown found a fourth nest, and, after watching as before, secured

the bird. We accidentally broke two of the eggs belonging to the third but reached Alexievka at midnight with fourteen identified grey plover's eggs. Two sittings were quite fresh, and made us an excellent omelette for breakfast the next morning. The other two were very slightly incubated."

For Seebohm and Harvie-Brown 22nd June 1875 certainly was a red-letter day—they had taken 162 or 164 eggs of eleven or twelve species, including a clutch of great snipe's eggs and another of little stint's. They had shot nine species of bird, including four grey plovers at the nest. Seebohm continues: "We spent the next two days in blowing our eggs and writing our journals, occasionally strolling out among the willows on the island to bag a few yellow-headed wagtails and other birds". A few days after these bloodthirsty adventures, after shooting eleven long-tailed skuas, they took two more clutches of grey plover's eggs and shot another adult bird. In all they took over a thousand eggs, twenty-eight of them grey plover's and they brought home over a thousand skins.

Nearly twenty years later Aubyn Trevor-Battye contrived to get himself to Kolguev Island and even to be cut off there by the ice. For him, too, collecting was more important than observation. On 26th June 1894 he writes as follows (1895):

> "Further on on the top of a wind-swept shoulder of the hill I took four eggs from a grey plover's nest. The nest was a deep circular depression containing, with the exception of a little lichen, nothing but the eggs. The hen bird I shot, but the male was impossible to secure, he was so wild and wary. After waiting about a long time for him I had to give it up."

In another clutch Trevor-Battye took on 13th July the eggs contained fully-formed young birds. He met with large flocks of grey plovers from 10th August onwards on the Kolguev mud flats—presumably the beginnings of the autumn migration.

As if the Kolguev grey plovers had not been sufficiently plundered in 1894 by Trevor-Battye, Henry J. Pearson (1899) and friends landed there in the following year and took "seven clutches of eggs and several young between July 7th and 13th". One clutch found on 9th July caused them some trouble in preserving. "The eggs were nearly hatching, and the young had their beaks through, calling distinctly; I could hear them several yards away". In the very same year another enthusiastic British egg-collector, H. L. Popham, took four clutches of grey plover's eggs at Golchicka on the River Yenesei. It was here that in 1914 Maud Haviland, who travelled with two women companions and "an American gentleman, Mr H. V. Hall, who was interested in the aborigines of Siberia", spent two months; and she is probably the last English ornithologist to have visited that area. She too was a collector, and the unfortunate grey plover was once again among the leading victims of destruction. She was just as capable as her male colleagues of taking and blowing eggs and shooting old birds at their nests. But at least she took a camera and obtained some remarkably good photographs of breeding waders; she also recorded the date of the departure of the grey plovers from their breeding grounds: 25th August.

Feeding grey plover, Humberside.

Not surprisingly, none of the ornithologists or oologists, as the egg-collectors preferred to call themselves, so far mentioned found out a great deal about the habits of the grey plover and, indeed, it remains a relatively little known bird. According to the *Birds of the Soviet Union* (Dement'ev 1969) grey plovers arrive singly on their breeding grounds and form pairs within a fortnight. The nest is a hollow scraped out in peaty soil; the four eggs are like those of the golden plover but lighter in tone. They are laid from mid-June onwards into July, but the incubation period is said to be unknown. A more recent manual, the *Handbuch der Vögel Mitteleuropas* (Glutz von Blotzheim 1975) adds some further scraps of information from North America sources and also mentions the longest-living grey plover so far recorded: a bird which carried its British ring for three weeks short of twelve years.

Autumn grey plovers displaying at each other.

In my part of the country, Humberside, the grey plover arrives in varying numbers every autumn and up to twenty or thirty are usually present at or near the Spurn Peninsula in winter. Here, I have on several occasions tried to photograph grey plovers on the open sandy shore, but with little success. The birds are extremely shy, refusing to approach near the hide. They can run quickly over the sand but, when feeding, a slow run or walk, between pauses standing stock-still, often on one leg, is the norm. At Spurn I have often watched a grey plover feeding with quick jabs and tugs of its bill on the slimy weed left stranded here and there by the tide; they also take small crabs, but their principal food is worms. Here, as elsewhere, each bird seems to hold a temporary winter feeding territory and can be found in the same spot for days in succession, and sometimes may be seen chasing away others of its kind.

In some autumns grey plovers can be quite numerous along both shores of the Humber inland as far at least as Barton and Hull. It was in October 1973 that I succeeded in photographing one which was to be found feeding day after day in a mud-filled clay-pit on the south shore of the Humber. I was able here to place my hide low down by the water's edge, partly hidden by a bank. Soon after I entered I heard the loud clear "clee-clee" or "pee-er-wee" whistle of the grey plover and the bird was soon feeding on the soft mud not far away. But here running was impossible. Its gait was of necessity slow, heavy and plodding; every time its foot was raised one could see that it was heavily clogged with mud. It frequently stood still, often leaning forward, evidently looking and listening, and occasionally it grabbed a worm. Once I saw it pull a quite fat ragworm, about three inches long, out of the mud with its bill. This bird approached to within nine metres of the hide—the closest I have ever been to a grey plover (p. 47 above).

Bird behaviour is often puzzling. At Gibraltar Point one autumn I watched two feeding grey plovers displaying, apparently aggressively or at least threateningly, at each other. The essential posture taken up by these birds was clear enough: legs bent somewhat, head bowed down so that the bill nearly touched the ground, wings flexed or partly outstretched, tail fanned. The behaviour lasted for some minutes, and was repeated. It always ended with one bird flying at and more or less chasing off the other. It seems reasonable to infer that these birds had taken up temporary feeding territories along the muddy tidal ditch where I had found them, and were defending these territories against each other (see previous page).

On the whole the grey plover is an exciting, not very common, rather shy and retiring bird about which considerably less is known than about any other of the plovers that regularly visit this country.

Lapwing flocks are typically composed of ten to fifty birds flying in a loose straggling group. Their slow-moving broad wings have a curious "wobbly" action which distinguishes a distant flying lapwing from a crow at a glance. ▶

CHAPTER ELEVEN

The Lapwing

THE familiar lapwing, which has had at least three books devoted to it (Ennion 1949, Spencer 1953 and Tolman 1969), is a common breeding bird throughout much of the Palaearctic from Spain to the Far East. Nowadays it breeds in the Faroes, Iceland, Shetland, Norway northwards to Finnmark, Sweden up to 65° 45' N, Finland, and in the Soviet Union across the Urals to the Yenesei and the Baikal Sea and as far as the River Ussuri on the far border of Manchuria near Vladivostok. In 1973 it nested in Japan. In the south the lapwing breeds around the Aral and Caspian Seas, in Iran, Turkey and northern Greece, northern Italy, Spain and Morocco.

Most authorities agree that the number of breeding lapwings in Europe declined in the second half of the nineteenth and the first quarter of the twentieth century because of the reclamation of much of their wasteland habitat. Climatic change and, in some areas, Britain perhaps especially, egging, may also have been important. But since the mid-twentieth century at the latest a remarkable recovery seems to have taken place in many parts of the range, the species having apparently taken increasingly to nesting on cultivated land. It has certainly begun to breed in new areas and increased substantially in number in many parts of its range. Thus in Belgium, breeding numbers are thought to have more than doubled in the last twenty-five years. In Luxembourg, where the lapwing had been extinct for thirty years, it has again bred since 1960 and numbers there had reached 200 pairs by 1973. One could be accused of frivolity for pointing out that, since 1971, the lapwing has colonized Liechtenstein; more significant is the recent extenstion of its range to northern Italy (Fantin 1971 and see Glutz von Blotzheim 1975), where it now seems to be quite widespread in the Po valley, but where it has also been nesting south of the Apennines in the province of Livorno. It seems to have been in the 1950s that this extension of the lapwing's breeding range began to take place, and it was further consolidated in the 1960s. In the south of France there is still only a single isolated breeding locality, in the Camargue, but elsewhere in that country the lapwing has been increasing in numbers.

The most spectacular extensions of the lapwing's range, which must surely be linked to climatic change, have taken place in the north. It has increased since the 1930s in northern Scotland and the Scottish islands. First recorded in the Faroes in 1935, it is now a regular breeding bird there, and it bred in Iceland in 1963 and 1964. Its spread northwards in Scandinavia has been notable. In Finland the northern limit of its breeding range has shifted some 700 or 800 km northwards since 1940. In Sweden there has also been a northward spread of the lapwing. In 1958 members of the Norwegian Ornithological Society were asked to fill in a questionnaire on the lapwing's breeding status in that country. The results showed that it had been steadily spreading northwards and inland in Norway since the beginning of the twentieth century (Myrberget 1962, Haftorn 1971), when the furthest north it reached was Røst and Bodø, not far north of the Arctic Circle. By 1935 lapwings were breeding on South Kvaløy near Tromsø, in 1940-1945 they reached Karlsøy north of Tromsø and in 1956-57 twelve pairs were nesting on Rolfsøy in Finnmark at 71° N, virtually the same latitude as the North Cape. At the same time they colonized inland areas of southern Norway and even began breeding on Dovrefjell, up to 2,700 feet above sea level, in 1936.

Although in general terms the lapwing is not a great migrant, yet it has become one of the most studied of all migrant birds (see especially Klomp 1947, Klomp and van der Starre 1956, Kluijver and van der Starre 1943 and

Imboden 1974). The pioneering Dutch work was based on the lapwing ringing station at Reeuwijk near Gouda run by J. and C. van der Starre on an island in a lake. Birds were caught on spring and autumn migration and not just ringed but also measured, weighed and their age and sex determined. By 1955 these indefatigable workers had ringed 10,000 lapwings since they began operations in 1938! They soon made some important discoveries. They found, for example, that while in the autumn some 50 per cent of lapwings were birds of the year, in the spring the proportion of juvenile lapwings was 40 per cent, indicating a higher winter mortality rate among the less experienced young birds. Curiously, they also found a preponderance of males—nearly 60 per cent of all the birds they caught were males, though there is no reason to believe that males are easier to catch than females.

Reeuwijk-ringed birds were recovered in winter in the south of France and the Iberian Peninsula and sometimes in Morocco; and in summer in the Baltic area, Scandinavia, Russia and Germany. This indicated that the lapwings breeding in much of central and northern Europe migrate westwards in the autumn through Holland. But Klomp showed that lapwings migrate in several stages. According to him, first, early summer migration in May-July into the alluvial areas of the Low Countries takes place; then there is a pause, while many of these birds moult; then a stage of "vagrant migration" follows in autumn when flocks tend to fly in different directions but not over great distances. Finally, when cold weather comes, the phenomenon known as "rush migration" occurs, when the lapwings migrate rapidly to their winter quarters in the south-west.

Equally exciting and innovatory was the much later work of the Swiss ornithologist Christoph Imboden (1974). His paper on lapwing migration was the first study to take into account all European recoveries of a single species, and one of the first to be based on analysis by computer. He collected together the 9,521 ringing recoveries of lapwings, 2,269 of them birds ringed as adults, from the 350,000 to 400,000 lapwings ringed between 1900 and August 1969. This represented a recovery rate of 2 or 2.5 per cent. Imboden divided European breeding lapwings into 14 different populations and mapped and described the migration of each. His figures show that the mean distance of recoveries over 60 kilometres away from the place of ringing is least in the French population and greatest among lapwings breeding in Finland. Thus 36-40 per cent of lapwings breeding in France are recovered within 60 kilometres of the place of ringing and the rest fly an average distance of 530 kilometres (young birds) or 400 kilometres (adults). Only 14 per cent of Finnish lapwings are recovered within 60 kilometres of the place or ringing, and the others fly an average distance of over 2,500 kilometres. The longest distances covered by migrating lapwings are revealed by birds ringed in their winter quarters in western Europe and subsequently recovered in the Soviet Union; Imboden recorded 4 cases of flights of over 5,000 kilometres by such birds. The longest flight of all was a bird ringed in the Basses-Pyrénées in January and recovered 1½ years later and 5,850 kilometres away in Novosibirsk. In over a dozen cases a lapwing was shown to have been migrating at a speed of over 100 kilometres per day. About 70 per cent of all lapwings return to their birthplaces in spring, leaving a mere 30 per cent free to colonize new areas.

Female lapwing injury feigning.

On one occasion at least lapwing migration has been actually observed and tracked on radar. On 31st January 1956, as reported by none other than the radar controller at Zürich airport (Hofmann 1956), an unidentified flying object was picked up on the radar screen at Kloten at about 1530 hours. It was moving at rather under 60 kilometres per hour at an altitude of 2,200 metres above sea level and failed to respond to attempts to make radio contact with it. A plane was sent up to make visual contact and discovered a 120-strong lapwing flock flying above a thick layer of cloud. They were tracked for over an hour flying in calm air in a west-south-west direction from over Stein-am-Rhein to near Olten and were evidently on a cold-weather flight, that is, part of the rush migration already mentioned.

The slow flying broad-winged lapwing is perhaps particularly liable to suffer from the natural hazards of weather during its migrations. Catastrophe struck an apparently resting flock of some 1,000 birds in the Eifel, near Dalhem in West Germany, in the evening of 19th July 1967. At least 300 of them were killed in a freak hailstorm, during which hail stones of at least an inch in diameter showered down on them and, in the case of some which were scientifically examined as corpses, actually broke their bones. Many others were so shocked and dazed or damaged that they fell easy victim to the birds of prey which gathered at the scene of disaster within a few days (Niethammer 1967).

In December 1927 another dramatic event affected at least one flock of migrating lapwings (Bagg 1967). Many of these birds apparently embarked on hard weather flights westwards or south-westwards from England and Wales or parts of the continent in mid-December 1927. But strong and persistent easterly winds swept some of them past or across Ireland and out over the Atlantic, and they arrived in numbers in Newfoundland. Weather maps showed that, especially on 20th December, strong easterly winds of at least 50 m.p.h. would have carried them all the way across the North Atlantic. The lapwing is probably the most sensitive of all birds to the onset of cold weather in winter, and its immediate response is to migrate westwards. Ireland is the mildest, but also the ultimate, place of refuge for them. In almost every winter, varying numbers of lapwings overshoot the mark and arrive in Iceland. Bagg showed that, from time to time, birds had crossed the Atlantic to North America in the same circumstances. He assembled all the North American records of lapwings up to 1966 and showed that they were concentrated in Newfoundland in November-January. There were 32 of them in all, relating to single birds except for the "great flight" of 1927, a smaller flight of at least 30 birds in January 1966, small groups in Newfoundland in September 1959 and January 1960, and a small flock in Bermuda in December 1956. The 1927 crossing was accomplished by several hundred lapwings in all; one of them, shot in Newfoundland on 27th December 1927, had been ringed as a chick at Ullswater in Cumbria, in the Lake District, in May 1926.

Lapwing behaviour has been the subject of numerous studies, some of them dealing with the autumn and winter period which so many ornithologists have neglected in favour of breeding season studies. Thus in Denmark Lind (1957) watched lapwings in September in the nature reserve at Tipperne in West Jutland and found that some of them at least, just like the grey plovers described earlier, were maintaining diminutive and evidently very temporary territories along the muddy shore. Used for feeding and defended against other lapwings, they were only a few metres across. Near these territories were non-territorial areas used for bathing, resting and preening. There were also flocks of non-territorial lapwings among which aggressive behaviour was seen similar to that between the territorial birds. I once watched an apparently serious fight between two lapwings in a flock on 30th October 1971. They stood face to face with outstretched wings and lunged at one another from time to time; they too were perhaps holding territories.

Two male lapwings in aerial display.

In the early 1920s R. H. Brown (1926) observed similar territorial behaviour among early autumn lapwing flocks in Cumbria. He noticed that some individuals were holding small territories "on the outskirts of the flock", and he thought they were held both by males and females, and that the males were occupying territories in order to display to the females. He repeatedly saw birds defending these territories adopting "an attitude of hostility, i.e. head lowered, body and tail elevated, wings rather open, often pecking at the ground and calling a shrill 'peet'". He also saw fights, "the combatants striking at one another with wings and feet, occasionally varying this by swooping at each other. Such fights often lasted intermittently for over half-an-hour." The male was triggered by the proximity of a female, and the implication was that males found mates in this way. Brown described this display as follows:

> ". . . it began with the male picking the grass, then scraping the ground with his feet and going forward on to his breast, which was moved up and down on the ground or else in a circular manner from right to left, whilst the wings were held wide apart and the tail elevated to show the bright tail-coverts. Usually the males uttered a shrill 'peet-peet-peet' during this display . . ."

The picturesque spring courtship of the lapwing has been described many times since Edmunds Selous's account appeared in 1905 in his book *Bird life glimpses*; in English for example by Brock in 1911, in Dutch by Rinkel in 1940, and most notably of all perhaps in German by Brunhilde Laven in 1941. Wife of H. Laven of ringed plover fame, she studied the lapwings breeding on the Courland Spit some 12-15 kilometres north of Rossitten, but a dense population of marauding crows rather vitiated her observations of the later stages of the lapwing's breeding cycle: she estimated that, mainly because of them, only 15 per cent of eggs laid hatched, and only 10 per cent of them produced fledged young.

From mid-February onwards the lapwings are to be found on their nesting grounds, the males taking up territories almost at once. Although solitary lapwing's nests are common, the birds usually breed in loose colonies or clusters, so that a quite small field may be divided into 3 or 4 territories and may later hold that number of nests. Cold or stormy weather may drive the lapwings off their nesting grounds for days at a time early in the season, and they often abandon the area for part of each day, especially the afternoon. The onset of laying is perhaps only indirectly linked to the weather; more directly to the food supply (Högstedt 1974). In Britain a completed clutch is seldom found before the end of March so that the birds normally spend a month or so on their territories before nesting proper begins.

The most spectacular and best known feature of the lapwing's breeding behaviour is the tumbling song flight of the male, heard from late February onwards at first mainly in the late evening and early morning, later at any time of day. The song flight appears to a human observer invariably to follow the same stereotyped and complex pattern; but no doubt the lapwing can readily distinguish between the songs of different individual males. The singing lapwing takes off from the ground with some rather slow, laboured, owl-like wing beats, flying low at first, then quickens the beat to gain height. One I watched began the first long drawn out rasping "carr" note of its song as it flew very low, followed by the next syllables "wee-ah-wee" or "pee-a-weet". Then it shot up some 30 feet or so almost vertically in silence, before flying along slowly, sometimes almost hovering, calling out the next part of the song, "a-weet-weet". This was followed by the dramatic tumbling dive during which the rest of the song was uttered, "pee-a-weet". Brock's rendering of the song is perhaps better than mine and certainly it is unusual: "whey—willuchoo ee—willuch—willuch— —cooee"; the tumbling dive coming before or at the same time as the last note. But the performance is still incomplete, for the lapwing also makes a loud buzzing noise with its outstretched primaries as it throws itself in flight first to one side and then to the other. Some lapwings regularly follow up their song with a series of these "buzzes", which are produced as the wing feathers are spread out and forced downwards. The buzzes are made in quite rapid succession—up to 2 or 3 per second—in brief spells of a few seconds' duration. Sometimes the wing buzzing is performed quite separately from the song flight, a bird flying up, buzzing its wings for a moment or two, then settling. When landing in its territory after a song flight, the male lapwing settles with a series of deliberate, slow wing beats and a glide. Each flight may last for up to five minutes non-stop, and include a whole succession of songs and wing buzzes, or it may last just long enough for a single song. I have seen a lapwing singing, with only a few brief intermissions on the ground, for over an hour at a time.

The exact function and nature of the lapwing's elaborate aerial song has yet to be elucidated. Is it primarily part of the mating process or has it a mainly territorial function? More puzzling still is another almost equally familiar phenomenon. Who has not noticed two lapwings rise into the air together? They fly side by side, up and down, for a time, sometimes almost touching. One dives at the other, which side slips out of the way. When they finally separate, after a flight of up to a minute or perhaps more, each often breaks into song as it swoops away. Though the song in these circumstances is incomplete it does indicate that these flights are undertaken by two males. But they are certainly not serious aerial combats; rather more like games, just play perhaps. Evidently male lapwings "enjoy" or "need" each other's company. Even on the ground they seldom fight, but frequently two neighbouring males can be seen standing face to face a few feet or yards apart. They draw themselves up to their full height and flex their wings slightly. When one moves a few paces, the other does the same. This performance often continues for several minutes.

A male lapwing in full song flight over the moors in April.

Male lapwings indulge in mild forms of territorial confrontation. Left, two males stand near each other with slightly flexed wings and upright stance.

As with other plovers, so with the lapwing, copulation is rarely seen and is over so quickly that only its later stages are usually noticed. It seems to occur "out of the blue", with no preparatory moves at all. On 9th April 1978 I watched a male fly directly after a brief song flight and alight on a female's back with a momentary quivering of his outstretched wings. He ran off almost immediately to his nearest scrape while the female called plaintively "pee-weet." So far as my observations go, coition never lasts longer than a few seconds and, more often than not, the male lands directly from flight on the female's back.

After leaving the scrape (left), the male lapwing pecks at pieces of grass, picks them up with his bill, and throws them behind him.

A male lapwing scraping (below). His breast is right down in the scrape, the black and white tail is well displayed, and the open bill shows that he is calling.

In five or six successive springs I have devoted many hours to lapwing-watching from a hide at two localities in North Humberside, and the most frequently observed courtship behaviour is undoubtedly the scraping ceremony. The male makes several scrapes and visits them from time to time. Using a special "hunched" run with lowered breast when he goes to a scrape, he starts flicking his tail up and down and going through pecking motions while straddling it. Then, settling into it, he begins to utter the special scraping call, a repeated rather rasping "co-co-co-co", which could also be rendered "zip-zip-zip" or "qua-qua-qua". While calling thus he bows rhythmically, his tail is flicked up and down, and then, supporting himself on his slightly opened wings, he goes down into the scrape and scrapes vigorously with his legs moving alternately, the call now rapidly repeated and more grating. Then he gets up, adopting a bowed posture, picks up pieces of grass with his bill and throws them behind him. A male may indulge time after time in this scraping, entirely on his own, with no female in attendance, but, sooner or later, if there is a female about she will be attracted, will run up to the scrape and, taking the male's place in it, will herself begin scraping vigorously. The male steps out of it on her approach and, pointing his bill and head directly downwards, raises his tail end straight up into the air, keeping his back to his mate in the scrape (p. 136 below). Both birds indulge in pecking movements, throwing grass fragments over their shoulders, when at the scrape and especially when leaving it.

The lapwing's four buff-coloured eggs, thickly speckled and mottled with dark brown and black, are surprisingly hard to see even on grass; they are often supremely well camouflaged when on plough. A colour-ringed female lapwing nested in four successive seasons in the same colony in Switzerland. Caught on 20th April 1960, which was St Hildegunde's day, she was affectionately known as "Hildegunde"; she was also F4459. She laid six clutches of four eggs in the four seasons, laying a replacement clutch in two seasons after losing the first clutch, but produced only five young in all. What was remarkable about Hildegunde was that her eggs seemed to match their immediate surroundings: a clutch of eggs near dead reeds had ochrous-coloured backgrounds, while in another near water the background colour of the eggs was bluish. One year, by artificially darkening the nest surroundings after he found it with three eggs, the author of this study, P. J. Heim (1962), was able to induce Hildegunde to lay a fourth egg darker than her first three Can the colour of a lapwing's egg possibly be affected by the nest-surroundings?

It seems ridiculous that, in this day and age, it is still perfectly lawful in Britain to take or destroy lapwing's eggs up till 15th April, but at least their sale and importation are banned. In the nineteenth century lapwing's eggs seem to have been a major food item, rather than just a delicacy, in Britain

(Cott 1953). They were certainly taken on a large scale and sold commercially; quantities of eggs reached the Leadenhall Market from East Anglia especially, but they were also imported from Ireland, Denmark and, above all Holland. The lapwing must have been at least locally an extremely abundant breeding bird in those days. A single egger was said to have taken nearly 2,000 eggs near Potter Heigham in Norfolk in a single season. On one estate near Thetford, according to C. B. Ticehurst, in the 1860s some 3,360 eggs were being taken annually; in the 1880s the annual number had fallen to 720, and no eggs were being taken after 1st May; in 1902 only 72 eggs were taken there, and in 1915 it was said that only 20 pairs of lapwings were nesting. Dr Cott's egg panel was invited to assess the relative acceptability of various eggs, some of which had been sold as plover's eggs: the scores were as follows:

lapwing	7.5
snipe	7.5
redshank	7.4
common tern	7.3
Sandwich tern	6.6
black-headed gull	6.6
rook	6.3

We have already had occasion to mention the Swiss ornithologist P. J. Heim in connection with the colour-ringed lapwing Hildegunde. He made an intensive study of a population of about 26 pairs of lapwings over a period of twenty-five years. They were nesting in some 70 acres of low-lying marshy ground at Nuolen on the left bank of the upper Lake of Zürich. On eight occasions in all those years Heim was lucky enough to find a nest containing a single freshly-laid egg and thereafter ascertain when exactly the subsequent eggs were laid. Normally, a lapwing lays one egg each day, he discovered, thus taking three days to complete the clutch. But, quite often, a gap of a day was left after the second or third egg, so that four days were required to complete the clutch. Heim was also able to establish the exact incubation period in the case of 22 eggs, and this worked out at 26-28 days; mean, 26.8 days. He also weighed the lapwing chicks and found that they began life weighing around 16.8 grams and put on weight at the rate of about 5 grams per day, so that by the time they flew at about 35-40 days old they weighed 170 grams (Heim 1959).

Ringing has shown that lapwings can live in the wild for 12, 14 or even 16½ years. Assuming that all lapwings breed in their first year, and many certainly do, then each pair has to raise 1.04 young each year to offset adult losses, which have been calculated from ringing data to be 34 per cent per annum (Boyd 1962).

CHAPTER TWELVE

Rare Visitors in Britain, Actual and Possible

THE PURPOSE of this final chapter is to give an account of those plovers which are rare vagrants only to Britain, as well as some of those which might be expected to occur here but have not. Of these rarer plovers, seven are definitely British birds. In the list that follows, the number of officially accepted records of each species up to and including 1978 is entered on the right (Rogers 1979).

lesser golden plover, *Pluvialis dominica* 56
semipalmated plover, *Charadrius semipalmatus*.......................1 (1978)
killdeer, *Charadrius vociferus*..25
sociable plover, *Chettusia gregaria* 22
Caspian plover, *Charadrius asiaticus*....................................1 (1890)
Greater sand plover, *Charadrius leschenaultii* 1 (1978)
white-tailed plover, *Chettusia leucura* 1 (1975)

To these seven species should be added some which might be expected to wander to Britain, or which have been recorded as doing so but are not yet officially accepted British birds. One distinct possibility is the lesser sand plover, *Charadrius mongolus*. The spur-winged plover, *Hoplopterus spinosus*, which breeds in Greece and has wandered to Germany, could also occur in Britain. Since the North American killdeer has occurred here, there is every reason to suppose that the piping plover, *Charadrius melodus*, whose breeding range overlaps that of the killdeer, might also cross the Atlantic to Britain, as has the semipalmated ringed plover, *Charadrius semipalmatus,* recently reported from the Scilly Isles, which breeds in the American Arctic south to Nova Scotia. The following key to the field identification of these rare plovers may be found useful.

I a Like golden plover but smaller, with relatively longer legs and long narrow wings; underwing greyish-brown not white, axillaries grey .... **lesser golden plover**
b Unlike golden plover ....see II

II a Like ringed plover, with or without black breast band.............................see III
b Unlike ringed plover. Lapwing-sized, rather long legs, wings with black tips .... see VI

III a Like ringed plover, but without black breast band .... see IV
b Like ringed plover with black breast band, or at least a black patch on either side of breast..see V

IV a Larger than ringed plover, brown above, white below, heavy black bill; male in summer with black mark through eye and broad but pale chestnut breast band which is faint and incomplete in winter .... **greater sand plover**
b Size as ringed plover, rather short tapering bill, plumage like greater sand plover .... **lesser sand plover**
c Size as ringed plover, no black on head, bright chestnut breast band in summer, faint brownish but complete breast band in winter .... **Caspian plover**

V a Indistinguishable in field from ringed plover but with more webbing between the toes...**semipalmated ringed plover**
b Size as ringed plover but much paler, especially the back, with narrow often incomplete black neck band .... **piping plover**
c Larger than ringed plover; two black breast bands in all plumages, chestnut rump, long tail, "kill-dee" call .... **killdeer**

VI a Rather smaller than lapwing, very black and white appearance, black cap, cheek and side of neck white, black line down centre of throat......... **spur-winged plover**
b Short white tail, long yellow legs, sandy grey or grey brown back and breast .... **white-tailed plover**
c Dark crown, white eye-stripe, tail white with black bar near tip...... **sociable plover**

A rare plover seen in Britain is most likely to be a lesser golden plover, which is divided into two sub-species, one in America, the other in Asia, from both of which populations individuals have wandered to Britain and the continent of Europe. Otherwise, it could be one of three North American species somewhat like our ringed plover, by far the most likely of these being the killdeer. Both the lesser golden plover and the killdeer have appeared, or at least been recorded, more often in recent years. Thus all but six of the fifty-six lesser golden plover records have been since 1962; now it is almost a regular, but still very scarce, autumn visitor. The killdeer usually turns up later; most records are from the winter or spring. It too has been occurring more frequently lately: only nine records up to the end of 1957, sixteen since then. The next most probable rare plover to be spotted again in Britain is the Asiatic lapwing-like sociable plover, which also usually turns up in the autumn; two other lapwing-like plovers are much less probable, the spur-winged and white-tailed plovers. The former has not yet been seen in Britain; the latter has turned up once only, in July 1975, at a Warwickshire gravel pit (Dean *et al.* 1977). Finally, of the three Asiatic sand plovers which might wander to Britain, the Caspian plover has done so once only, nearly a century ago; and the greater sand plover has recently been reported.

Not all the species so far mentioned will be given extended treatment in what follows: the white-tailed plover has been considered in Chapter One; the semipalmated ringed plover is indistinguishable in nearly all respects from the ringed plover, and some authorities regard it as a sub-species only. This leaves us with the lesser golden plover, the sociable and spur-winged plovers, the killdeer and the piping plover, and the three sand plovers.

Our European golden plover is a less widespread and less numerous bird than the apparently more successful lesser golden plover, which breeds on the tundra eastwards from the Yamal Peninsula to the Bering Straits and thence into Alaska and Arctic North America. The ranges of the two sub-species, *Pluvialis dominica dominica* in North America and *Pluvialis dominica fulva* in Asia, overlap in western Alaska, where intermediate birds occur. The two sub-species, both of which resemble the so-called "northern" race of the golden plover in summer plumage, were not generally regarded as distinguishable in the field until in 1978 the *British Birds* Rarities Committee (Rogers *et al.* 1978) apparently found that, after all, this was possible, and, without further explanation, they attributed most of the astonishing total of six records in 1977 to one or other sub-species (3 *dominica*, 1 *fulva*, 2 uncertain). Most of the British and other European records before then are of indeterminate sub-species. Indeed for the British Isles up to 1971 there were only three definite records of *fulva*, the Asiatic or Pacific golden plover, all from the late nineteenth century, two from England and one from Scotland, and two Irish records of *dominica*. On the European mainland, the American golden plover seems never to have been definitely identified; the only certain examples being from offshore islands: Heligoland 1847, two first year birds trapped on 20th December; Ushant, off the Breton coast, in September 1966. Otherwise the American golden plover has been proved to wander to this side of the Atlantic only twice, in 1924 and 1966, when single birds were identified in the Cape Verde Islands off the African coast.

As against the half dozen or fewer certain occurrences of the American golden plover in Europe, the Asiatic bird has been identified relatively often in or near Europe—in Tunisia, Algeria, Malta (four times), Italy, Spain, Sweden, Norway and even Greenland. While the few West German records of *fulva,* like the British ones already mentioned, date from the nineteenth century, twelve of the fifteen Dutch records (of trapped birds) are from the twentieth century though mostly from before 1920.

In many important respects the lesser golden plover resembles the golden plover. But, whereas the golden plover breeds commonly far south of the Arctic, for example in Britain, the lesser golden plover is confined to the tundra. Unlike the golden plover, too, it is a long-distance migrant. The adult American golden plovers fly south-west from their Alaskan and Arctic Canadian breeding grounds, passing through Labrador and thence out over the Atlantic southwards. A few stop momentarily in the Lesser Antilles or Bermuda; most apparently fly over 2,400 miles of open ocean until they reach the coast of Brazil. But their phenomenal migratory flight by no means finishes there, for they press on southwards for some 3,000 more miles overland, to reach their wintering grounds in the Argentine pampas. Their return flight in the spring is by a quite different mainly overland route of about 8,000 miles, for they migrate northwards through Central America, across the Gulf of Mexico and up the Mississippi valley. It is this overland route which is apparently followed by the juvenile birds on their first autumn migration southwards.

A bathing lapwing (below and left) dips its wings into the water and shakes itself vigorously, spraying the water in all directions. To dry its wings it jumps up a foot or two into the air and beats or vibrates them extremely rapidly, causing a momentary whirring noise. The speed of this action may be judged by the fact that these exposures were made at 1/1000 second, which has caught the water droplets in mid-air but not "frozen" the lapwing's wings.

The migration of the Asiatic golden plover is, if anything, even more remarkable than that of the American sub-species, making this bird well deserving of its name "Pacific". From the tundras of north-eastern Siberia these birds undertake enormous trans-oceanic flights to south-east Asia, Australia, Tasmania and New Zealand. Incredibly, too, they make their way to hundreds of scattered islands throughout the Pacific, including Hawaii, the Tuamotu Archipelago and the Tonga Islands, while others may be found on the coasts of Japan, China and India.

When in 1962 E. M. Nicholson and James Ferguson-Lees showed that a whole series of rare birds allegedly killed or found dead in the Hastings area of Sussex may not have been genuine stragglers to this country, and recommended that these so-called "Hastings rarities" be expunged from the official record of British birds, the sociable plover was one of the worst affected species. At that time there had been ten occurrences in Britain, three of which had to be scrubbed from the record. Unlike any of the other records, before or since, these alleged Hastings records of sociable plovers, purportedly from Romney Marsh and Winchelsea, were of small flocks of birds: six in May 1907, five in May 1910, and three in May 1914. Not only has the sociable plovers very seldom turned up in Europe more than one at a time in one place, but it has not very often been recorded in May. Of the twenty-two British and Irish records accepted up to 1978 all were in July-January, with October birds predominating, except for one in April and one in May.

The sociable plover is a migrant, breeding in the open steppes of southern Central Asia, north of the Caspian and Aral Seas, especially in Kazakhstan and western Siberia, and wintering in north-east Africa, southern Arabia, Iraq and India. On at least eighty occasions it has strayed to central, western or northern Europe as far as Spain, Ireland and Finland, turning up in every month of the year, but especially in March-April and October-November. Very often these sociable plovers have occurred in lapwing flocks, and it has been suggested that they may have been drawn off course, as it were, by the lapwings. In just the same way the lesser golden plovers recorded in Holland have almost always occurred among golden plovers; they too were probably diverted from their normal migration route after inadvertently joining a flock of golden plovers.

Like a pale, brownish-grey lapwing with no crest or dark back and somewhat longer legs, the sociable plover tends to adopt a more upright stance than the lapwing, which holds its body more horizontally. Its dark cap and conspicuous white or cream eyestripe and its black-grey legs distinguish it at all times of year from the otherwise rather similar white-tailed plover. In flight the tail pattern, white with a broad black band near the tip, is similar to the lapwing's, and quite different from the white-tailed plover's, which is white, and the spur-winged plover's, which is mostly black.

Formerly much more widespread than it is now, the sociable plover has declined dramatically in numbers as a result of the reclamation of much of its steppe breeding habitat. It nests in loose colonies of from three to fifteen pairs, often in the neighbourhood of water. The nest is at first a virtually unlined scrape, but is soon more or less filled with pieces of grass and other vegetation and small stones, in which the eggs are sometimes two-thirds hidden. The normal clutch is four, but clutches of five are not very rare. Thus in the Naurzum reserve in northern Kazakhstan, of 66 nests examined, 12 had clutches of five and 54 had clutches of four eggs. The eggs themselves are virtually indistinguishable from those of the lapwing.

The sociable plover in flight is said to resemble the stone curlew more than the lapwing; but its feeding behaviour very much resembles that of the lapwing, even to the extent of a similar foot-trembling routine. Its food is mainly insects, especially beetles and grasshoppers, and some vegetable matter.

Unlike the sociable plover, the spur-winged plover is not on the British list. On the other hand it was found breeding in Europe in 1959, when a group of Dutch ornithologists located nests both in Greece and in European Turkey (Ferguson-Lees 1965 and Vader 1965). It had long been known to breed in Asiatic Turkey, and its breeding range includes Syria, Jordan, Israel, Egypt, East Africa south to the equator, and Africa westwards south of the Sahara to Senegal. While southern populations appear to be sedentary, northern ones apparently migrate south to overwinter in Egypt. Records outside the breeding range have been few and far between. Birds have "overshot the mark" on spring migration to appear in April-May in the Ukraine (1837), near Burgas in Bulgaria (1962), in West Germany (1964 and 1978), in Jugoslavia on three occasions (1857, 1885, 1901), and in the south of Spain (1856). Deviations on autumn migration probably account for the August and October records in Romania (1964), at Arta in south-west Greece (1968), and in Malta (1865). On this basis the species may never wander as far as Britain, but at least British ornithologists have much less far to travel to see this fine bird in its native haunts than they have to see any of the others described in this chapter.

The Council of Europe's conservation committee claimed in 1972 that "between 20 and 50 pairs" of spur-winged plovers were breeding in Europe; in 1975 the authors of the *Handbuch der Vögel Mitteleuropas* were prepared to go further, and estimated a grand total of 50-100 pairs on the European side of the Aegean. There seems little doubt that the species has extended its breeding range and increased in number in northern Greece since its first discovery there, even though these events coincided with an increase in the number of ornithologists visiting this area, many of them specifically searching for spur-winged plovers. Thus in 1959 one party of ornithologists found one spur-winged plover's nest at Porto Lago; in 1960 two separate ornithologists found two separate nests there; in 1961 one of them returned with a group of companions and three nests were found at Porto Lago.

Ferguson-Lees (1965) suggested that the colonization of parts of the north Greek coast by spur-winged plovers had probably taken place in the 1950s, though "odd pairs may well have bred in Greece in the past". It is quite possible, however, that the nineteenth-century records from Euboea and Attica were connected with breeding in Thrace and Macedonia and even that the records mentioned above, from that period, may have been connected with an earlier phase of expansion (Glutz von Blotzheim 1975).

The spur-winged plover is reminiscent of a rather small, long-legged lapwing with a plain sandy brown back and very striking black and white head and underparts. In flight it shows a mainly black tail, but white upper tail coverts. It has less white on the wing than either the sociable or the white-tailed plover, though the black and white pattern is similar in all three species, the wing tips being black in all three. Its call, which is uttered a great deal during the breeding season, has been rendered in colloquial English "did ye do it" or "did ye see 'im do it", and in German "charadlio" or "charadidlio". This appears to be the note written down by Ferguson-Lees as "zic-zac-zac".

As a breeding bird the spur-winged plover seems to be equally at home along the coast, especially at river mouths, along rivers, on the shores of inland lakes, or on cultivated land preferably near water or at least periodically flooded. Brackish water seems to be favoured. The nest is a scrape in mud or sand, sometimes lined quite thickly, but usually with little lining, and the eggs are like those of the lapwing in colour, but smaller and less pointed. Normal clutch size appears to be four but clutches of two, three and five eggs have been recorded, and it has been suggested that there is a tendency for northern clutches to be larger than southern: clutches of two eggs are only mentioned from the south of the range, clutches of five only from the north (Glutz von Blotzheim 1975).

Either to keep its eggs cool in hot weather or to prevent them drying out, a spur-winged plover has been seen to wet its breast and belly feathers by dipping them into a pool of water before taking its turn to incubate (Crossley 1964). To the same end, a bird has been watched settling over the eggs on its tarsi so as to allow a draught to play over them while they are kept shaded. It has also been found that incubation is very irregular during the day and continuous only at night, in the early morning and late evening. The spur-winged plover's diet consists chiefly of insects.

Should you happen to see a ringed plover which is much too big to be a ringed plover and is therefore not a ringed plover, it will almost certainly prove to be that rare American visitor the killdeer, so named from its call. Look more closely and its unmistakable field characters will be apparent: two narrow black breast bands one above the other, orange-buff rump, long white-edged tail, long straw-coloured legs, and black beak.

In 1976 three separate killdeers were spotted in Britain, bringing the grand total of occurrences in Britain and Ireland to twenty-three. The killdeer has also turned up in Hawaii, Greenland, Iceland, the Azores, Madeira, France (1954 and 1972), Sweden (1968), and Switzerland (1974 and 1977). In a large part of the southern United States it is a resident; birds breeding further north in the northern United States and in southern Canada migrate southwards to winter in Central and South America and in the West Indies.

The killdeer is a conspicuous, noisy and beautiful bird which is well known and loved throughout its North American breeding range. It nests commonly near human habitation, either in cultivated fields, pastures, or on bare gravelly ground, often not very far from water. Nests have been found on gravel drives and even between the sleepers of a railway, and once on the tarred roof of a racetrack grandstand. The male killdeer in spring marks out its chosen territory with a remarkable song flight which may continue for many minutes at a time. The bird flies to and fro, round and round, above a restricted area, calling loudly and melodiously "killdeer, killdeer", sometimes flying so high as to be out of sight. Apart from this more developed and evidently more often indulged in song flight, the killdeer's breeding behaviour does not seem to differ very much from the ringed plover's, though its broken-wing distraction display, accompanied often by a fanning out of the depressed tail to display the conspicuous orange rump, seems to be more frequent than the ringed plover's.

The piping plover is another American bird which might be expected some day to cross the Atlantic, though apparently it has not yet done so. It migrates up and down the east coast of the United States. About ringed plover size, the adult in summer has a bill coloured like a ringed plover's, black bars on the forehead and breast, and a black collar, but it is much paler than the ringed plover and the black markings are much smaller. In winter and juvenile plumage the sexes are similar and there are no black markings at all; separation from the Kentish plover might then be difficult, but the piping plover is larger than the Kentish and has yellowish, not blackish, legs.

The piping plover nests on the sandy shores of the Atlantic coast of the United States as far south as North Carolina; also along the shores of lakes, including the Great Lakes, into southern Canada. It winters on the southern Atlantic and Gulf coasts of the United States and to some extent in the West Indies. One of its best-known characteristics is its clear melodious whistling call "peep, peep, peeplo", which often reveals its presence before it has actually been seen. The nest is a slight hollow in the sand, sometimes lined with small stones, and the birds tend to breed in small colonies. The piping plover feeds on larvae, insects, small molluscs and marine worms.

The last group of birds to be dealt with in this chapter are the three Asiatic sand plovers, two of which, the Caspian plover and the greater sand plover, have strayed here on one occasion. On 22nd May 1890 the male of an apparent pair of Caspian plovers was shot on the North Denes golf course, Great Yarmouth, Norfolk (Riviere 1930). The Caspian plover very seldom wanders out of its normal range in the direction of Europe and it is noteworthy that nearly all the records are old ones. They are as follows (Glutz von Blotzheim 1975):

Ukraine, near Odessa, 1836	1
Bulgaria, 1879	1
Malta, March 1911, September 1966, July 1968	3
Italy, November 1887, November 1898	2
West Germany, Heligoland, November 1850, May 1859	2
Britain, Norfolk, May 1890	1
Total number of occurrences	10

Lapwing courtship. As the female lapwing begins to settle in the scrape the male leaves it and raises his tail end up in the air, displaying his orange under tail coverts to his mate.

There are two geographically separate races or sub-species of the Caspian plover. *Charadrius asiaticus asiaticus* breeds round the northern and western shores of the Caspian Sea, round the Aral Sea, and locally in Kazakhstan, and winters in the Persian Gulf, eastern and southern Africa. *C.a. veredus* breeds in Mongolia, northern China and Korea and winters in South-East Asia and Australasia.

The Caspian plover is by no means an easy bird to identify, mainly because of its similarity to the Mongolian or lesser sand plover. All three sand plovers have similar plumage, but the greater sand plover *Charadrius leschenaultii* is much larger than the other two, being about the size of a turnstone while the other two sand plovers are no larger than the familiar ringed plover. All three differ from the other *Charadrius* plovers in having no white collar and long legs. The Caspian plover stands fairly upright, not unlike a golden plover, has a longish bill for its size, and its folded wings project beyond the tip of its tail. This last character, if visible, is distinctive, because in the other two sand plovers the folded wing and tail appear to be about the same length. It is sometimes said that, in spring, the Caspian plover can be distinguished from the other two sand plovers by its conspicuous chestnut breast band (those of the other two sand plovers are markedly less bright) bordered with black along the lower edge. This is certainly true of the male, but in the female the chestnut is considerably less bright and the black border is reduced or even almost non-existent, so that in this respect it can closely resemble the adult male lesser sand plover in breeding plumage. In all plumages it seems that the Caspian plover has more white on the forehead and above the eye than either of the other two species (Wallace 1973 and Reynolds 1972, but, above all, Glutz von Blotzheim 1975).

The Caspian plover's note has been described as a short sharp "quit". It breeds in dry or marshy areas of uncultivated steppe and also frequents river and lake shores and grassy pastures. Eggs are laid from mid-April onwards; the clutch is three and the eggs are less pointed than those of most other *Charadrius* plovers and similar to the dotterel's in appearance as well as shape.

Of the two other sand plovers, usually known as the greater and lesser, one, the greater, has occurred once in Britain. Its breeding range extends from around the southern half of the Caspian Sea eastwards across central Asia to the Altai, Mongolia and the Gobi Desert. In recent years, however, isolated breeding populations have been discovered in Iran, Afghanistan, central Turkey, northern Syria and northern Jordan; it has also apparently nested more than once in Somalia.

Unlike the Caspian plover, which winters inland, the greater sand plover winters along the coast of Africa, India and the Arabian Peninsula. In Europe there had been only two records before 1951, one in Greece in 1900 and the other in Sweden in June 1938, but since then there has been a spate of records, which should have alerted British ornithologists to the possibility of the bird occurring here. Sure enough on 9th December 1978, one was found at Pagham Harbour, Sussex, where it obligingly stayed until 1st January 1979. At the last detailed count, made in 1975, the recorded European occurrences of the greater sand plover since 1950 were as follows:

Ukraine, May 1951	1
Greece, August 1954, September 1954 (6 birds)	2
Sweden, August 1954, May 1961	2
France, Camargue, June 1969, May 1970	2
Malta, August 1972	1
Total number of occurrences	8

The greater sand plover should be separable from the lesser sand plover by its size alone, but the long heavy bill is also an important character (Wallace 1973, Williams 1963, and Sinclair and Nicholls 1980). The black markings round the eye and forehead, white throat, broad rusty red breast band of the summer plumage, as well as its white wing bar and outer tail feathers, are all shared with the lesser sand plover. It is not at all clear how the calls differ, if they do, from the lesser sand plover's, nor is enough known of the breeding habits of the two species to establish how they differ. Both lay clutches of three eggs and nest on open sandy or stony flats and semi-desert areas. Both species feed mainly on insects.

The lesser sand plover *Charadrius mongolus* is also known as the Mongolian sand plover. It is an undersized version of the greater sand plover; its short thick bill may also help to distinguish it from that species. It is much more of an eastern species than the greater sand plover or Caspian plover, breeding in two distinct areas, one in the far north-eastern corner of Asia, the other in central Asia eastwards from Tien Shan and the Pamirs. In much of its range it is a bird of the high mountains; it winters in the same area as the greater sand plover but does not reach so far south. Odd birds have appeared west of its normal range: on the Aral Sea in May 1953, in Syria in May 1904, in Cyprus in April 1957 and 1958, and in Turkey in May 1876. To Europe the lesser sand plover has strayed once only: on 17th September 1964 one was identified in the delta of the Rhine, in Austria, at the southern end of the Lake of Constance.

Bibliography

General

Bannerman, D. A. 1961. *The birds of the British Isles,* 10. London.
Boyd, H. 1962. "Mortality and fertility of European Charadrii." *Ibis,* 104: 368-87.
Dement'ev, G. P. *et al.* 1969. *Birds of the Soviet Union,* 3. Jerusalem.
Glutz von Blotzheim, U. N. *et al.* 1975. *Handbuch der Vögel Mitteleuropas,* 6. Wiesbaden.
Haftorn, S. 1971. *Norges fugler,* Oslo.
Lippens, L. and Wille, H. 1972. *Atlas des oiseaux de Belgique et d'Europe occidental,* Tielt.
Parslow, J. 1973. *Breeding birds of Britain and Ireland,* Berkhamstead.
Peterson, R. T. 1934. *A field guide to the Birds,* Boston.
Peterson, R. T. *et al.* 1954. *A field guide to the birds of Britain and Europe,* London.
Rosenberg, E. 1967. *Fåglar i Sverige,* Stockholm.
Salomonsen, F. 1967. *Fuglene på Grønland,* Copenhagen.
Sharrock, J. T. R. 1976. *The atlas of breeding birds in Britain and Ireland,* B.T.O., Tring.
Snow, D. W. (ed.). 1971. *The status of birds in Britain and Ireland,* B.O.U., Oxford.
Witherby, H. F. *et al.* 1943-44. *The handbook of British birds,* 5 vols. London.
Voous, K. 1960. *Atlas of European birds,* London.
Yeatman, L. 1976. *Atlas des oiseaux nicheurs en France,* Paris.

Chapter One The World's Plovers

Austin, O. L. 1963. *Birds of the world,* London.
Bock, W. J. 1958. "A generic review of the plovers" (*Charadriinae, Aves*). *Bulletin of the Museum of Comparative Zoology,* 118(2): 27-97.
Campbell, B. 1974. *The dictionary of birds in colour,* London.
Hall, K. R. L. 1960. "Egg-covering by the white-fronted sand plover. *Charadrius marginatus.*" *Ibis,* 102: 545-53.

Chapter Two Plovers in History, Literature and Legend

Baugh, A. C. 1963. *Chaucer's major poetry,* Fifth edition. New York.
Bewick, T. 1821. *A history of British birds,* 1. Fifth edition. Newcastle.
Clarke, H. and Carter, A. 1977. "Excavations in King's Lynn, 1963-70." *Society for Medieval Archeology,* 7.
Evans, A. H. 1903. *Turner on birds,* Cambridge.

Gurney, J. H. 1921. *Early annals of ornithology*, London.

Platt, C. and Coleman-Smith, R. 1975. *Excavations in medieval Southampton*, 1953-69. 2 vols. Leicester.

Ray, J. 1678. *The ornithology of Francis Willughby*, English version of the *Ornithologia*, first published 1676. London.

Society of Antiquaries. 1975. "Excavations at Portchester Castle. Saxon." *Report of the Research Committee*, 33(2).

Spencer, K. G. 1953. *The lapwing in Britain*, London.

Stevenson, H. 1870. *The birds of Norfolk*, 2. London.

Swainson, C. 1885. *Provincial names and folklore of British birds*, English Dialect Society. London.

Wilson, D. M. (ed.). 1976. *The archeology of Anglo-Saxon England*, London.

Yapp, W. B. 1979. "Birds in English medieval manuscripts." *Journal of Medieval History*, 5: 315-348.

Yarrell, W. 1871-85. *British birds*, 4 vols. Revised edition. London.

Chapter Three Plumage and Field Identification

Appleton, G. F. and Minton, C. D. T. 1978., "The primary moult of the lapwing." *Bird Study*, 25:253-6.

Bisson, A. J. 1969. "Golden plovers with wing-bars." *British Birds*, 62:233-4.

Fjeldså, J. 1977. *Guide to the young of European precocial birds*, Tisvilde.

Minton, C. D. T. 1977. "Wader plumages in autumn and winter." *British Birds*, 70:521-9.

Prater, A. J. *et al.* 1977. *Guide to the identification and ageing of Holarctic waders*, B.T.O., Tring.

Snow, D. and B. 1976. "Post-breeding moult of the lapwing." *Bird Study*, 23:117-20.

Wynne-Edwards, V. C. 1957. "The so-called 'Northern Golden Plover'." *Scottish Naturalist*, 69:89-93.

Chapter Four Ecology and Food

Bringeland, R. 1965. "Temporaere dverglobiotoper." *Sterna*, 6:281-95.

Collinge, W. E. 1924-7. *Food of some British wild birds*, York.

Elgmork, K. 1962. "Dverglo hekker ved ferskvann på Østlandet." *Sterna*, 5:133-6.

Holt, C. W. 1947. "Pattering action of lapwing when feeding." *British Birds*, 40: 125.

Hori, J. 1962. "Waders being caught by cockles and mussels." *British Birds*, 55:443-4.

Imboden, C. 1971a. "Bestand, Verbreitung und Biotop des Kiebitz in der Schweiz." *Der Ornithologische Beobachter*, 68:37-53.

Imboden, C. 1971b. "Der Biotop des Kiebitz in der Schweiz." *Revue Suisse de Zoologie*, 78:578-86.

Johnson, W. 1947. "Pattering action of Lapwing when feeding." *British Birds*, 40:349.

Källander, H. 1977. "Piracy by Black-headed Gulls on Lapwings." *Bird Study*, 24:186-94.

Klomp, H. 1953. "De terreinkeus van de kievit." Leiden. Reprinted 1954 in *Ardea*, 42:1-139.

Lister, M.D. 1964. "The Lapwing habitat enquiry," 1960-1. *Bird Study*, 11:128-47.

Lloyd, D. 1977. "Golden plover survey." *B.T.O. News*, 89.

Nicholson, E. M. 1938 and 1939. "Report on the Lapwing Habitat Inquiry," 1937. *British Birds*, 32:170-91 and 207-9; 33:255-9.

Selous, E. 1927. *Realities of bird life*, London.

Simmons, K. E. L. 1961a. "Foot-movements in plovers and other birds." *British Birds*, 54:34-9.

Simmons, K. E. L. 1961b. "Further observations on foot movements in plovers and other birds. *British Birds*, 54:418-22.

Sluiters, J. E. 1954. "Waarnemingen over de drie bij Amsterdam broedende pluviersoorten", *Limosa*, 27:71-86.

Chapter Five The Kentish Plover

Alexander, H. G. 1974. *Seventy years of birdwatching*, London.

Kearton, R. 1899. *Our rarer British breeding birds*, London.

Rittinghaus, H. 1961. *Der Seeregenpfeifer*, Wittenberg Lutherstadt.

Smith, A. E. and Cornwallis, R. K., 1955. *The birds of Lincolnshire*, Lincoln.

Chapter Six The Ringed Plover

Clapham, C. 1978. "The Ringed Plover populations of Morecambe Bay." *Bird Study*, 25:175-80.

Edwards, G. *et al.* 1947. "Aggressive display of the Ringed Plover." *British Birds*, 40:12-19.

Laven, H. 1940. "Beiträge zur Biologie des Sandregenpfeifers." *Journal für Ornithologie* 88:183-287.

Marples, G. 1931. "Experimental studies of the Ringed Plover. The retrieving, recognition, orientation and rotation of its eggs by the bird." *British Birds*, 25:34-44.

Mason, A. G. 1947. "Territory in the Ringed Plover." *British Birds*, 40:60-70.

Prater, A. J. 1973. "Plovers pose problems." *B.T.O. News*, 57.

Prater, A.J. 1976. "Breeding population of the Ringed Plover in Britain." *Bird Study*, 23:155-61.

Regnell, S. 1965. "Kort bidrag till kännedomen om större strandpiparens häckningsbiologi." *Vår Fagelwärld*, 24:310-13.

Simmons, K. E. L. 1953. "Some aspects of the aggressive behaviour of three closely related plovers (*Charadrius*)." *Ibis*, 95:115-27.

Smith, N. G. 1969. "Polymorphism in ringed plovers." *Ibis*, 111:177-88.

Vaurie, C. 1964. "Systematic notes on palaearctic birds, 53. Charadriidae: the genera *Charadrius* and *Pluvialis*." *American Museum Novitates* 2177.

Walters, J. 1956. "Eirückgewinnung und Nistplatzorientierung bei See-und Flussregenpfeifer." *Limosa*, 29:103-29.

Williamson, K. 1947. "The distraction display of the ringed plover." *Ibis*, 89:511-13.

Chapter Seven The Little Ringed Plover

Armstrong, E. A. 1952. "The distraction displays of the Little Ringed Plover and territorial competition with the Ringed Plover." *British Birds*, 45:55-9.

Dathe, H. 1953. *Der Flussregenpfeifer*. Wittenberg Lutherstadt.

Durango, S. 1943. "Några iakttagelser av den mindre strandpiparen." *Fauna och Flora*, 1943:145-54.

England, M. D. *et al.* 1944. "The breeding of the Little Ringed Plover in England in 1944." *British Birds*, 38:102-11.

Gatter, W. 1971. "Wassertransport beim Flussregenpfeifer." *Vogelwelt*, 92:100-3.

Hölzinger, J. 1975. "Verhalten und Nahrungsgrundlage des Flussregenpfeifers in Wasser-führenden und wasserlosen Brutrevieren." *Der Ornithologische Beobachter*, 72:9-17.

Hölzinger, J. and Schilhansl, K. 1972. "Untersuchungen zur Brutbiologie an einer südwest-deutschen Population des Flussregenpfeifers." *Beiträge zur naturkundlichen Forschung Südwest-Deutschlands*, 31:93-101.

Ledlie, R. C. B. and Pedler, E. G. B. 1938. "First breeding of Little Ringed Plover in Britain." *British Birds*, 32:90-102.

Parrinder, E. D. 1969. "Little Ringed and Ringed Plovers laying in the same nest." *British Birds*, 62:233.

Parrinder, E. R. 1950. "The Little Ringed Plover in Great Britain in 1949." *British Birds*, 43:279-84.

Parrinder, E. R. 1952. "The Little Ringed Plover in Great Britain in 1950." *British Birds*, 45:61-4.

Parrinder, E. R. 1954. "The Little Ringed Plover in Great Britain. 1951-3." *British Birds*, 47:198-203.

Parrinder, E. R. 1957. "The Little Ringed Plover in Great Britain. 1954-6." *British Birds*, 50:365-71.

Parrinder, E. R. 1960. "The Little Ringed Plover in Great Britain during 1957-9." *British Birds*, 53:545-53.

Parrinder, E. R. 1964. "Little Ringed Plovers in Britain during 1960-2." *British Birds*, 62:219-23.

Parrinder, E. R. and E. D. 1969. "Little Ringed Plovers in Britain in 1963-7." *British Birds*, 62:219-23.

Rosenberg, N. T. and Nielsen, B. P. 1957. "Iagttagelser af vadefugle, isaer af Lille Praestekrave ved Sondersø, Nordsjaelland," 1954. *Dansk Ornithologisk Forenings Tidsskrift*, 57:65-73.

Simmons, K. E. L. 1953. "Some studies on the little ringed plover." *Avicultural Magazine*, 59:181-207.

Simmons, K. E. L. 1955. "The significance of voice in the behaviour of the Little Ringed and Kentish Plovers." *British Birds*, 48:106-15.

Simmons, K. E. L. 1956. "Territory in the little ringed plover." *Ibis*, 98:390-7.

Sluiters, J. E. 1938. "Bijdrage tot de biologie van den Kleinen Plevier." *Ardea*, 27:123-51.

Stein, F. 1958. "Zur Biologie des Flussregenpfeifers." *Beiträge zur Vogelkunde*, 6:311-39.

Walters, J. 1957. "Über den Balzruf des Flussrengenpfeifers." *Ardea*, 45:62-72.
Walters, J. 1961. "Notes on the chicks of the Little Ringed Plover." *Bird Study*, 8:15-18.
Wyss, H. 1946. "Beobachtungen an brütenden Flussregenpfeifern." *Der Ornithologische Beobachter*, 43:61-71.

Chapter Eight The Dotterel

Berg, B. 1924. *Min vän fjällpiparen*, New edition, Stockholm.
Carlo, E. A. di and Heinze, J. 1978. "La nidificazione del piviere tortolino sugli Appennini." *Rivista Italiana di Ornitologia*, (2) 48:149-56.
Carlo, E. A. di and Heinze, J. 1979. "Il piviere tortolino come uccello di passo e nidificante in Italia." *Gli Uccelli d'Italia*, 47-69.
Carlo, E. A. di and Heinze, J. 1979. "La nidificazione del piviere tortolino in Italia." *Gli Uccelli d'Italia*, 159-174.
Haviland, M. D. 1917-18. "Notes on the breeding habits of the dotterel on the Yenesei." *British Birds*, 11:6-11.
Heyder, R. 1960. "Die Südereale des Mornellregenpfeifers in Europa." *Abhandlungen und Berichte aus dem Staatliche Museum für Tierkunde in Dresden*, 25:47-50.
Heyder, R. 1962. "Nachlese zur Verbreitung und Biologie des Mornell-regenpfeifers." *Abhandlungen und Berichte aus dem Staatlichen Museum für Tierkunde in Dresden*, 26:103-11.
Marra, N. 1965. "Nieuwe broedgevallen van de Morinelplevier in Oostelijk Flevoland," *Limosa*, 38:2-5.
Mears, C. S. 1917-18. "Field notes on the nesting of the dotterel in Scotland." *British Birds*, 11:12-14.
Nethersole-Thompson, D. 1973. *The dotterel*, London.
Rittinghaus, H. 1962. "Untersuchungen zur Biologie des Mornellregenpfeifers in Schwedisch-Lappland." *Zeitschrift für Tierpsychologie*, 19:539-58.
Vaughan, R. 1952. "Accertata nidificazione sul Massicio della Maiella (Abruzzi) del piviere tortolino." *Rivista Italiana di Ornitologia*, (2)22.
Vaughan, R. 1953. "Alcune osservazioni su gli uccelli del Massicio della Majella (Abruzzi)." *Rivista Italiana di Ornitologia*, (2) 23:137-42.

Chapter Nine The Golden Plover

Byrkjedal, I. 1974. "Heiloen som hekkefugle in Rogaland." *Sterna*, 13:1-13.
Eenhuistra, O. 1973. *Goudplevier en wilstervangst*, Fryske Academy. Leeuwarden.
Fuller R. J. and Youngman, R. E., 1979. "The utilisation of farmland by golden plover wintering in southern England." *Bird Study*, 26:37-46.
Haverschmidt, F. 1943. "De Goudplevierenvangst in Nederland." *Ardea*, 32:35-74.
Hudson, R. 1965. "Summary of foreign-ringed birds in Britain and Ireland during 1906-63." *British Birds*, 58:87-97.
Lloyd, D. 1977 and 1978. "Golden plover survey." *B.T.O. News*, 89 and 95.
Part, R. 1979. "Sequential breeding by golden plovers". *British Birds*, 72:499-503.

Ratcliffe, D. 1976. "Observations on the breeding of the Golden Plover in Great Britain." *Bird Study*, 23:63-116.
Rittinghaus, H. 1969. "Ein Beitrag zur Okologie und Verhalten des Goldregenpfeifer zu Beginn der Brutzeit." *Die Vogelwarte*, 25:57-65.
Ruttledge, R. F. 1966. *Ireland's birds*, London.
Speek, B. J. 1973. "Ringverslag van het vogeltrekstation. 1911-1970." *Limosa*, 46:109-35.
Steiniger, F. 1959. *Die grossen Regenpfeifer*, Wittenberg Lutherstadt.
Williamson, K. 1948. "Field notes on the golden plover." *Ibis*, 90:90-8.
Yalden, D. W. 1974. "The status of the Golden Plover and Dunlin in the Peak District." *The Naturalist*, 930:81-91.
Youngman, R. and Fuller, R. 1976. "Wintering golden plovers." *B.T.O. News*, 81.

Chapter Ten The Grey Plover

Branson, N. J. B. A. and Minton, C. D. T. 1976. "Moult, measurements and migrations of the grey plover." *Bird Study*, 23:257-66.
Dathe, H. 1949. "Der Kiebitzregenpfeifer in Sachsen." *Beiträge zur Vogelkunde*, 1:54-97.
Haviland, M. D. 1915. *A summer on the Yenesei*, London.
Haviland, M. D. 1915. "Notes on the grey plover on the Yenesei." *British Birds*, 9:162-6.
Meise, W. 1952. "Über Zug und Mauser des Kiebitzregenpfeifer." *Beiträge zur Vogelkunde*, 2:137-51.
Nisbet, I. C. T. 1957. "Wader migration at Cambridge Sewage Farm." *Bird Study*, 4:131-48.
Pearson, H. J. 1899. *Beyond Petsora eastward*, London.
Prater, A. J. 1971, 1972, 1973, 1974. "Estuary bird survey." *B.T.O. News*, 46, 52, 60, and 66.
Seebohm, H. 1901. *The birds of Siberia*, London.
Trevor-Battye, A. 1895. *Ice-bound on Kolguev*, London.

Chapter Eleven The Lapwing

Bagg, A. M. 1967. "Factors affecting the occurrence of the Eurasian lapwing in eastern North America." *The Living Bird*, 6:87-121.
Brock, S. E. 1911. "Lapwings in the pairing season." *The Zoologist* (4)15:296-304.
Brown, R. H. 1926. "Some breeding habits of the Lapwing." *British Birds*, 20:162-8.
Cott, H. B. 1953 and 1954. "The exploitation of wild birds for their eggs." *Ibis*, 95:409-49 and 643-75, and 96:129-49.
Ennion, E.A.R. 1949. *The Lapwing*, London.
Fantin, G. 1971. "La pavoncella fa il nido in Italia." *Rivista Italiana di Ornitologia*, 41:390-400.
Heim, P. J. 1959. "Gewichtszunahme von Jungkiebitzen bei natürlichen Aufwachsen." *Der Ornithologische Beobachter*, 56:2-8.
Heim, P. J. 1962. "Beobachtungen an einem farbberingten Kiebitzweibchen." *Der Ornithologische Beobachter*, 59:65-9.
Heim, P. J. 1974. "Eiablage, Gelegegrösse und Brutdauer beim Kiebitz." *Der Ornithologische Beobachter*, 71:283-8.

Hofmann, H. 1956. "Kiebitze auf dem Radarshirm." *Der Orthnithologische Beobachter,* 53:79-81.
Högstedt, G. 1974. "Length of the pre-laying period in the lapwing in relation to its food resources." *Ornis Scandinavica,* 5:1-4.
Imboden, C. 1974. "Zug, Fremdansiedlung und Brutperiode des Kiebitz in Europa." *Der Ornithologische Beobachter,* 71:5-134.
Klomp, H. 1947. "Verslag van het Kievitenringstation 'Reeuwijk' over de jaren 1943-5 en gegevens over de trek van de Kievit." *Limosa,* 19:76-117.
Klomp, H. and van der Starre, C. 1956. "Verslag van het Kievitenring-station 'Reeuwijk' over de jaren 1946-55." *Ardea,* 44:269-81.
Kluijver, H. N. and van der Starre, C., 1943. "Verslag van het Kievitenringstation te Reeuwijk over de jaren 1938-42." *Ardea,* 32:264-72.
Laven, B. 1941. "Beobachtungen über Balz und Brut beim Kiebitz." *Journal für Ornithologie,* 89:1-64.
Lind, H. 1957. "Territorial opførsel hos vibe om efteröret." *Dansk Ornithologisk Forenings, Tidsskrift,* 51:22-9.
Myrberget, S. 1962. "Vipas utbredelse i Norge." *Sterna,* 5:1-4.
Niethammer, G. 1967. "Hagel erschlägt Kiebitze." *Die Vogelwarte,* 24:107-9.
Rinkel, G. L. 1940. "Waarnemingen over het gedrag van de Kievit gedurende de broedtijd." *Ardea,* 29:108-47.
Selous, E. 1905. *Bird life glimpses,* London.
Ticehurst, C. B. 1932. *A history of the birds of Suffolk.* London.
Tolman, R. 1969. *De kievet. Een monographie over onze nationale vogel.* Baarn.

Chapter Twelve Rare Visitors to Britain, actual and possible

Crossley, R. 1964. "Spur-winged plovers wetting their feathers before incubation." *British Birds,* 57:515-16.
Dean, A. R. *et al.* 1977. "White-tailed Plover: new to Britain and Ireland." *British Birds,* 70:465-71.
Ferguson-Lees, I. J. 1965. "Studies of less familiar birds, 132. Spur-winged Plover." *British Birds,* 58:45-7 (with plates).
Nicholson, E. M. and Ferguson-Lees, I. J. 1962. "The Hastings rarities." *British Birds,* 55:299-384.
Reynolds, J. F. 1972. "Photographs of immature Caspian Plovers." *British Birds,* 65:124-5.
Riviere, B. B. 1930. *The birds of Norfolk.* London.
Rogers, M. J. *et al.* 1978. "Report on rare birds in Great Britain in 1977." *British Birds,* 71:481-532.
Rogers, M. J. *et al.* 1979. "Report on rare birds in Great Britain in 1978." *British Birds,* 72:503-49.
Sinclair, J. C. and Nicholls, G. H. 1980. "Winter identification of greater and lesser sand plovers." *British Birds,* 73:206-13.
Vader, W. J. M. 1965. "The first nesting of Spur-winged Plover in Greece." *British Birds,* 58:195-6.
Wallace, D. I. M. 1973. "Identification of some scarce or difficult west Palearctic species in Iran." *British Birds,* 66:376-90.
Williams, J. G. 1963. *A field guide to the birds of East and Central Africa,* London.

Index